FINANCIAL
PLANNING USING
SPREADSHEETS

THE FINANCIAL SKILLS SERIES

The rapidly changing role of the finance function in modern organizations is creating greater and more varied demands on the skills of everyone involved in the world of finance and accounting. To enable busy professionals to keep up with the pace of change, Kogan Page has joined forces with the Chartered Institute of Management Accountants (CIMA) to create an up-to-the-minute series of books on financial skills.

Highly practical in nature, each book is packed with expert advice and information on a specific financial skill, while the lively style adopted reflects the current dynamism of the discipline.

Published titles in the series include:

Cost Control: A Strategic Guide
David Doyle

Quality in the Finance Function
David Lynch

Implementing an Accounting System
A Practical Guide
Revised edition
Ray Franks

Strategic Financial Decisions
David Allen

Investment Appraisal
A Guide for Managers
Second edition
Rob Dixon

Financial Modelling for Business
Decisions
Bryan Kefford

Financial Planning
Modelling Methods and Techniques
Second edition
David Asch and G. Roland Kaye

An Introduction to Strategic
Financial Management
The Key to Long Term Profitability
David Allen

Financial Planning Using
Spreadsheets
Forecasting, Planning & Budgeting
Techniques
Sue Nugus

Forthcoming:
Activity Based Costing
John Innes and Falconer Mitchell

For further information on the series, please contact the Marketing department at Kogan Page, 120 Pentonville Road, London N1 9JN, Tel. 0171 278 0433, Fax 0171 837 6348. CIMA members can also contact the Publishing Department at the Institute.

FINANCIAL
PLANNING USING
SPREADSHEETS
FORECASTING, PLANNING & BUDGETING TECHNIQUES

Sue Nugus

The Chartered Institute of
Management Accountants

**KOGAN
PAGE**

YOURS TO HAVE AND TO HOLD

BUT NOT TO COPY

First published in 1997

Kogan Page Limited
120 Pentonville Road
London N1 9JN

© TechTrans Limited, 1997

British Library Cataloguing in Publication Data

A CIP record for this book is available from the British Library.

ISBN 0 7494 2567 9

Typeset by TechTrans Limited, Kidmore End, Oxfordshire
Printed in England by Clays Ltd, St Ives plc

Contents

About the Author

Sue Nugus is a consultant and author with more than fifteen years in the IT industry. During this period her main concern has been in the field of ensuring that information systems users have been able to use the technology to enhance their personal performance and to this end she has designed and conducted training courses which have been offered in Europe, Asia, Africa and Australia. She regularly consults on information systems problems and has recently become involved in working with organisations on how to take most advantage of the World Wide Web. Among her many clients Sue has worked extensively with the Chartered Institute of Management Accountants and the Institute of Chartered Accountants in England and Wales. She has authored and co-authored some twenty books on a range of IT subjects that have been published by McGraw-Hill, NCC-Blackwell and Butterworth Heinemann.

Email address: consult@techtrans.i-way.co.uk

Preface

The objective of this book is to help spreadsheet users improve their skills by providing a structured approach to developing spreadsheets for forecasting, financial planning and budgeting.

The book assumes that the reader is familiar with the basic operation of a Windows spreadsheet and is not intended for beginners. Every endeavour has been made to make this book package independent and inevitably there are some issues that cannot be achieved in all the current spreadsheets and when this has occurred in the book it will be indicated. The two principal packages that have been referenced are Microsoft Excel and Lotus 1-2-3 as these are generally recognised as the leading Windows spreadsheets.

Formulae and command descriptions are referenced without package specific prefixes when the formula is otherwise the same for both Excel and 1-2-3. However if the logic or construction of a formula or command is different, entries have been given for both Microsoft Excel and Lotus 1-2-3.

The screen shots in the book have generally been created using Microsoft Excel and 1-2-3 screen shots have also been included where the procedure being described is different.

Readers using a different Windows spreadsheet will find that the techniques explained in the book are equally relevant, although it is possible that some command sequences might be slightly different.

The book has been divided into three parts covering the areas of Forecasting, Planning and Budgeting separately. Although it is recommended that readers follow the book from the beginning, the text is also intended as a reference book that will be a valuable aid during model development.

The disk that accompanies the book contains all the examples described in both Excel and 1-2-3 format. Instructions for installing and using the disk are supplied on the disk itself and it is recommended that readers consult the README file contained on the disk.

Introduction

The maxim, 'managing means looking ahead', gives some idea of the importance attached to planning in the business world, and it is true that if foresight is not the whole of management at least it is an essential part of it.

H. Fayol, *General and Industrial Management*, Pitman, London, 1949.

Financial forecasting, planning and budgeting are sometimes grouped together and the question *'what is the real difference?'* is asked. They are in fact distinctly different activities and to a large extent require different spreadsheet techniques.

FORECASTING

A forecast is a prediction of what is expected to occur in the future. A business forecast is thus a prediction or estimate of future sales, prices, inventory levels, etc. Forecasts can vary in the way they are presented and the amount of detail that is produced. For example the sales forecast may be stated as a total of so many millions of units or may be broken down by product line or by geographical area.

An important issue concerning business forecasting is that the forecaster often does not have operating responsibility for achieving the forecast and in this case the forecast is primarily a passive statement.

PLANNING

There are many different types of business plans, including profit and loss plans, cash flow plans and capital plans, and indeed they tend to focus on a particular business objective such as profit, return on investment or cash flow. However, whatever the type of plan, it can be seen as a statement of how a particular activity, process or project is intended to proceed.

Plans often incorporate forecast data, but will then include more detail by showing, for example, what resources will be allocated in order to achieve the forecast.

Although like those involved in producing forecasts, planners do not always have operating responsibility for achieving the proposed outcome of the plan, they will usually have to have the plan agreed by those who will be responsible for its operation. Therefore a plan is not as passive as a forecast.

BUDGETING

A budget can be defined as a detailed estimate of future transactions. It can be expressed in terms of physical quantities, financial terms, or both. The essence of a budget is that it is a target set for management to achieve or surpass. Thus a budget is always associated with a responsibility point or centre within the organisation. For example the marketing division may have a sales budget, a factory might have a capital budget or an individual may have an expenses budget. Whatever the case there will always be an identifiable person or team responsible for achieving the budget. For this reason a budget may be seen as being active as opposed to passive.

FORECASTING, PLANNING AND BUDGETING

A sales forecast is always the first step in the cycle. It will sometimes supply little detail, stating perhaps only the number of units that will be sold in a given period.

A planner will then take the forecast and add to it some of the detail required for a budget, but will usually not be the person with operating responsibility for the budget.

When the figures generated by the plan have been accepted by management into the organisations' specific operating targets responsible individuals or teams are then identified.

Of course, a key difference in the approach to budgeting as opposed to forecasting and planning is that a financial budgetary system should provide the organisation with a mechanism for the effective management of the enterprise. Forecasts and business plans, on the other hand, are rarely called upon to provide such a level of working detail.

Well-designed and implemented budgetary systems can deliver enormous benefits to the organisation and should be seen as both a management tool and a fundamental philosophy with which the business is conducted.

SUMMARY

This book considers the three activities of forecasting, planning and budgeting in turn.

In the forecasting section a series of approaches to forecasting are explained which range from smoothing techniques to regression analysis and time series analysis. In the planning section different approaches to developing plans including deterministic, stochastic and optimising will be explained and examples of how to go about developing these types of plans will be given. In addition, this section will cover the spreadsheet techniques available for what-if analysis, risk analysis and goal seeking. The final section of the book considers different approaches to using a spreadsheet for budgetary control. This section illustrates when it is appropriate to work with single files as opposed to linking multiple files and examples are given.

$$\boxed{1}$$

Part One

Forecasting

INTRODUCTION

The objective of a business forecast is to predict or estimate a
future activity level such as demand, sales volume, asset
requirements, inventory turnover, etc. It relies on the analysis of
historic and/or current data to produce these estimates. The more
accurate business forecasts are, the more efficient and effective an
organisation can strive to be.

Before trying to decide on an appropriate forecasting technique
it is important to collect as much data and information as possible
and to examine this data to look for trends, seasonal fluctuations,
business cycles, etc. How to do this is explained in Chapter 2.
Chapters 3 through 6 will then consider a range of possible
forecasting techniques that can be applied and in Chapter 7 how to

select the most appropriate technique for the type and quantity of data available is described.

APPROACHES TO FORECASTING

There are different approaches to forecasting, and these can be categorised in a number of different ways. One of the more common forecast categories is time, i.e. how far into the future is a forecast designed to look. In this case there can be *short-term* forecasts, *medium-term* forecasts, and *long-term* forecasts. The time-span a forecast is considered to fall in will depend on the circumstances and the type of industry involved. In general business terms, short-term forecasts would involve periods of up to one year, medium-term forecasts would consider periods of between one and five years and long-term forecasts would be for longer periods.

Another form of categorisation is *objective* or *quantitative* forecasts and *subjective* or *qualitative* forecasts.

Subjective forecasts

Subjective or qualitative forecasts rely to a large extent on human input and an in-depth knowledge of the activity being forecast. It may be prepared by reading reports and by consulting experts for information and then using this information in a relatively unspecified or unstructured way to predict the required activity. A forecasting method discussed in Chapter 6, called the *composite of individual estimations*, is based on essentially subjective information. The main disadvantage to this approach is that there is no clear methodology which can be analysed to test how a forecast may be improved in order that past mistakes are avoided. Subjective forecasting does not usually require much mathematical input and thus a spreadsheet will play an accompanying role as opposed to a central role in the production of such forecasts.

Objective forecasts

An objective, or quantitative approach to forecasting requires a model to be developed which represents the relationships deduced from the observation of one or more different variables. This is generally achieved by recording historic data and using these historical facts to hypothesise a relationship between the items to be forecast and the factors believed to be affecting it. Because the objective approach requires the use of mathematical models to describe and analyse the relationships between the variables, the spreadsheet is an ideal tool and thus can play a central role in the production of such forecasts.

Objective forecasting methods are sometimes considered to be more dependable than subjective methods because objective methods are less affected by what the forecasters would like the result to be. Furthermore forecasting models can incorporate means of assessing the accuracy of the forecast and adjusting the data to produce more accurate figures in the future.

Of course, it is important to appreciate that there has to be an element of subjectivity in all forecasting techniques. At the end of the day what the forecasters know about the business will affect the choice of a particular forecasting technique, and subsequently their knowledge is likely to affect how the forecast data is used to predict activity within the organisation.

Forecast units

Whether forecasts are categorised in terms of time or level of objectivity, the forecast unit is also an important variable. For example a forecast might seek to estimate the level of sales, either as sales units or as sales revenue; or a forecast might seek to establish a level of probability such as a service level of 99%. It might be appropriate to forecast activity levels such as the numbers of customer service enquiries that are expected between 10am and 11am.

Finally, any forecast must also be seen in terms of whether it is a once-off estimation or a repetitive calculation. Once-off forecasts are normally concerned with large projects and thus may be performed with the aid of considerable financial resources. Repetitive forecasts are usually required for situations where there is a need for ongoing adjustments to previously forecast figures. These forecasts must be developed in such a way that actual data can be entered into the model in order to assess the accuracy of the forecast and for adjustments to be made in order to attempt to make the next forecast more accurate.

Collecting and Examining the Data

Without systematic measurements, managers have little to guide their actions other than their own experience and judgment. Of course, these will always be important; but as businesses becomes more complex and global in their scope, its becomes increasingly more difficult to rely on intuition alone.

J. Singleton, E. McLean and E. Altman, Measuring information systems performance: Experience with the management by results system at Security Pacific Bank, *MIS Quarterly*, June 1988.

DATA COLLECTION

Before selecting a forecasting technique it is important to collect an appropriate amount of data on which to base the forecast. The actual amount and type of data that constitutes 'appropriate' will vary depending on the activity to be forecast. However, it is important to consider at what point historic data is no longer relevant. In a business environment data older than five to ten years would normally be considered suspect.

The historic data should be examined to ascertain the presence of any obvious patterns. For example is there evidence of trend, seasonality or business cycle? Of course the amount of data will also affect which types of patterns can be sought. For example, in order to establish the presence of seasonality a sufficient number of periods of data must be available, and business cycles can only be considered by looking at a large number of periods. The data can be found on the CD accompanying this book under the name **RAWDATA**.

First draw a graph

The data shown in the following examples represents historic sales data from which forecasts are to be produced. In order to simplify the examination of the data, line graphs have been produced. This is a good example of using simple graphs to look at spreadsheet data which immediately illustrates the presence or absence of patterns in the data that would otherwise require careful mathematical analysis of a set of numbers.

No trend or seasonality

The first data set in Figure 2.1 shows 24 months of historic sales units. By looking at the graph in Figure 2.2 it is clear that there is no strong trend, no apparent seasonality and the number of periods are too few to be able to perceive a business cycle. Based on these observations the next period is as likely to increase, decrease or remain the same.

HISTORIC MONTHLY SALES DATA FOR 1996/97

1996	JAN	FEB	MAR	APR	MAY	JUN	JUL	AUG	SEP	OCT	NOV	DEC
Sales Volume	63	57	59	48	55	61	61	45	54	68	56	66

1997	JAN	FEB	MAR	APR	MAY	JUN	JUL	AUG	SEP	OCT	NOV	DEC
Sales Volume	70	59	60	70	72	62	65	58	56	68	65	63

Figure 2.1 Historic data for 24 monthly periods showing no trend

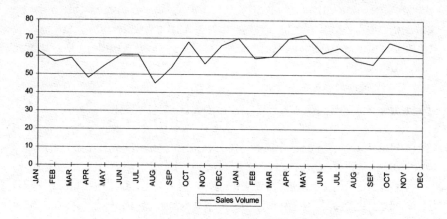

Figure 2.2 Graphical output for data showing no trend

Some evidence of trend

Figure 2.3 represents another set of 24 months of historic sales data. From the graph in Figure 2.4 it can be seen that looking across the 24 periods the sales are increasing, although there are fluctuations in the data. This would indicate an upward trend. Of course, a trend may not always be favourable and it is important to be able to explain the reason for any trend; for example growth in the market, success of a marketing plan, or perhaps an increase in costs is causing a downward trend.

HISTORIC MONTHLY SALES DATA FOR 1996/97

1996	JAN	FEB	MAR	APR	MAY	JUN	JUL	AUG	SEP	OCT	NOV	DEC
Sales Volume	57	59	61	59	63	65	69	65	73	75	70	80

1997	JAN	FEB	MAR	APR	MAY	JUN	JUL	AUG	SEP	OCT	NOV	DEC
Sales Volume	85	90	92	94	96	80	93	95	88	97	98	99

Figure 2.3 Historic data for 24 monthly periods showing some trend

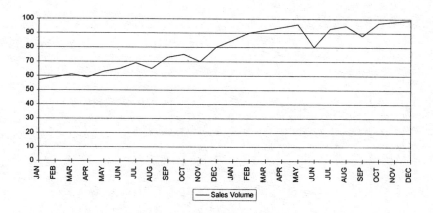

Figure 2.4 Graphical output for data showing some trend

Seasonality

The data in Figure 2.5, which is shown graphically in Figure 2.6, suggests a strong indication of seasonality. By examining the data displayed graphically in Figure 2.6 it can be seen that there appears to be a similar peak in the data between June and September for both years, which might indicate a seasonal pattern. To confirm this it would be important to refer back to the item being forecast to ensure that this is indeed the case.

HISTORIC MONTHLY SALES DATA FOR 1996/97

1996	JAN	FEB	MAR	APR	MAY	JUN	JUL	AUG	SEP	OCT	NOV	DEC
Sales Volume	25	28	30	35	31	33	49	30	33	35	35	43

1997	JAN	FEB	MAR	APR	MAY	JUN	JUL	AUG	SEP	OCT	NOV	DEC
Sales Volume	33	35	36	40	33	37	50	42	38	35	43	49

Figure 2.5 Historic data for 24 monthly periods showing some seasonality

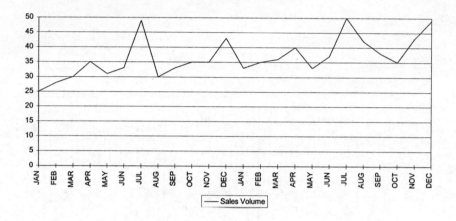

Figure 2.6 Graphical output for data showing some seasonality

Business cycle

The last set of data to be examined here is shown in Figure 2.7 and consists of quarterly sales data for a 26 year period. Figure 2.8 shows the data graphically and by studying the graph there appears to be a five year cyclical pattern to the data. As a business cycle implies a cyclical trend pattern over a longer period of time, the data in this example might, for example, refer to the sale of houses and further investigation could show that the five yearly peaks and troughs correspond with interest or inflation rates.

HISTORIC QUARTERLY SALES DATA IN MILLIONs FOR 1969/1994

Sales Volume	QRT 1	QRT 2	QRT 3	QRT 4	QRT 1	QRT 2	QRT 3	QRT 4
QUARTERS - 1969/	90.49	80.35	88.49	94.17	91.16	85.26	90.00	84.80
QUARTERS - 1971/	82.05	78.64	77.03	72.23	77.20	78.84	73.37	79.90
QUARTERS - 1973/	74.28	74.28	74.28	74.28	74.28	74.28	74.28	74.28
QUARTERS - 1975/	84.36	93.02	96.14	85.38	93.42	81.71	88.55	89.86
QUARTERS - 1977/	86.68	83.24	79.08	79.31	74.34	76.06	78.19	69.27
QUARTERS - 1979/	75.00	80.25	85.33	86.33	88.63	94.01	94.51	95.01
QUARTERS - 1981/	95.11	105.10	97.09	108.21	110.78	95.22	112.49	108.26
QUARTERS - 1983/	102.35	98.20	96.40	94.86	91.12	94.93	88.97	83.22
QUARTERS - 1985/	81.59	82.82	94.64	92.54	84.22	88.37	93.68	94.75
QUARTERS - 1987/	97.09	100.04	100.48	104.09	103.84	111.73	101.66	110.17
QUARTERS - 1989/	99.58	104.44	97.63	95.51	94.91	89.96	85.31	89.27
QUARTERS - 1991/	83.95	88.48	80.78	86.68	93.12	82.55	94.97	93.52
QUARTERS - 1993/	93.78	96.87	95.63	98.73	107.16	100.65	110.96	105.50

Figure 2.7 Quarterly data for 26 years indicating a business cycle

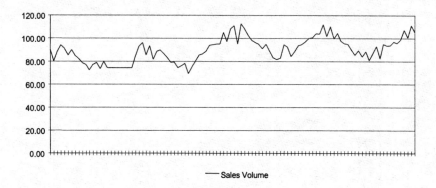

Figure 2.8 Graphical output for data indicating a business cycle

USING STATISTICAL MEASURES

As well as examining data visually for trend and seasonality, it is also important to be able to describe or summarise the data using statistical measures.

Descriptive statistics

The descriptive statistics included here are the *mean*, the *mode*, the *median*, the *standard deviation*, the *variance* and the *range*.

Figure 2.9 shows 100 observations that represent sample production weights of a product such as cereals, produced in grams. This data is the *sample data* from which the descriptive statistics are measured. The term *sample* is important as it implies that the data does not represent the full *population* and this affects some of the spreadsheet functions used. A population is the complete data set from which a conclusion is to be made.

The data, which can be found on the CD accompanying this book under the name **DESCRIP**, has been entered onto Sheet A and the range A3 through L22 has been named DATA.

	A	B	C	D	E	F	G
1	100 OBSERVATIONS PRODUCTION WEIGHTS IN GRAMS						
2							
3	525	539	580	563	497		
4	499	594	594	569	555		
5	548	588	502	516	540		
6	568	516	550	562	556		
7	555	562	548	548	546		
8	549	576	560	498	554		
9	562	553	575	539	531		
10	586	567	509	529	587		
11	596	577	574	555	580		
12	569	550	557	558	563		
13	562	519	569	530	560		
14	567	553	524	501	512		
15	558	593	558	539	588		
16	563	599	543	512	550		
17	564	579	581	546	534		
18	559	531	521	505	556		
19	559	542	587	574	533		
20	580	580	561	551	512		
21	551	523	529	548	502		
22	585	579	536	540	570		
23							

Figure 2.9 100 observations of production weights in grams

The mean, median and mode are described as *measures of central tendency* and offer different ways of presenting a typical or representative value of a group of values. The range, the standard deviation and the variance are *measures of dispersion* and refer to the degree to which the observations in a given data set are spread about the arithmetic mean. The mean is the most frequently used measure of central tendency, and statisticians to describe a data set frequently use the mean together with the standard deviation. Figure 2.10 shows the result of the descriptive statistic functions which can be found on Sheet B of the file DESCRIP. Each statistic is explained in detail below.

	A	B
1	Results of Descriptive Statistics	
2		
3	Number of Observations	100.00
4	Mean	552.30
5	Median	555.00
6	Mode	580.00
7	Minimum	497.00
8	Maximum	599.00
9	Range	102.00
10	Standard Deviation	25.14
11	Variance	631.83
12		

Figure 2.10 Results of descriptive statistics

Mean

The *mean* or *arithmetic mean* is defined as follows:

$$\text{sample mean} = \frac{\text{total of a number of sample values}}{\text{the number of sample values}}$$

To calculate the sample arithmetic mean of the production weights the AVERAGE[1] function is used as follows in cell B4.

In Excel:

=AVERAGE(DATA)

In 1-2-3:

@AVG(DATA)

---

[1] It is important to note that the AVERAGE function totals the cells containing values and divides by the number of cells that contain values. In certain situations this may not produce the required results and it might be necessary to ensure that zero has been entered in order that the function sees the cell as containing a value.

Sample median

The *sample median* is defined as the middle value when the data values are ranked in increasing, or decreasing, order of magnitude. The following formula in cell B5 uses the MEDIAN function to calculate the median value for the production weights:

MEDIAN(DATA)

Sample mode

The sample mode is defined as the value which occurs most frequently. In Excel there is a built-in MODE function, but in 1-2-3 it is necessary to calculate the mode. The following Excel formula is required to calculate the mode of the production weights.

In Excel:

MODE(DATA)

The mode may not be unique, as there can be more than one most frequently occurring value. Furthermore, if every value in the sample data set is different, there is no mode.

In 1-2-3 where there is no formula, it would be necessary to write a macro that identifies the most frequently occurring measure.

Minimum and maximum

It is useful to know the smallest and the largest value in a data series and the MINIMUM and MAXIMUM functions have been used in cells B6 and B7 to calculate this as follows:

MIN(DATA)

MAX(DATA)

The range

The range is defined as the difference between the largest and smallest values in a data series. The following formula can be used to calculate the range of the production weights by referencing the already calculated minimum and maximum values:

B7–B6

Sample standard deviation

The sample standard deviation s is obtained by summing the squares of the differences between each value and the sample mean, dividing by $n - 1$, and then taking the square root. Therefore the algebraic formula for the sample standard deviation is:

$$s = \sqrt{\frac{\sum x^2 - \frac{(\sum x)^2}{n}}{n-1}}$$

In other words the standard deviation is the square root of the variance of all individual values from the mean. The more variation in the data, the higher the standard deviation will be. If there is no variation at all, the standard deviation will be zero. It can never be negative.

To calculate the standard deviation for the production weights the following standard deviation function is required in cell B9:

In Excel:

STDEV(DATA)

In 1-2-3:

STDS(DATA)

Note that both the above functions assume a sample population. If the data represents the entire population then in Excel the function STDEVP() would be used and in 1-2-3 the required function would be STD().

Sample variance

The sample variance is the square of the standard deviation. The formula required to calculate the sample variance of the production weights data in cell B10 is:

In Excel:

VAR(DATA)

In 1-2-3:

VARS(DATA)

In the same way as the standard deviation, the above functions assume that sample data is being use. For the entire population the functions VARP() and VAR() respectively are required.

SUMMARY

The first step in preparing any forecasting system is to carefully examine the available data in order to ascertain the presence of a trend, a seasonal pattern or a business cycle. It is then useful to prepare a set of descriptive statistics such as those described in this chapter in order to embark on an appropriate forecasting technique with useful information about the original data.

3

Smoothing Techniques

Good judgment is usually the result of experience. And experience is frequently the result of bad judgment.

R. E. Neustadt and E. R. May, *Thinking in Time*, The Free Press, New York, 1986.

INTRODUCTION

Smoothing techniques are a means of establishing future estimated values by calculating various types of averages.

Estimating a single value for the next period is called *univariate analysis* and there are a number of techniques that can be used to produce the forecast value. These include:

1. estimation of the value;
2. using the last known value;
3. calculating the average or arithmetic mean of the historic data.

Estimation of the value is a subjective approach that depends entirely on the forecaster knowing the business and being able to judge the outcome for the next period. In some cases this is referred to as *guesstimation*.

In a situation where the examination of the historic data has shown no evidence of a trend then using the last known value can be an appropriate method of estimation.

Using an average or arithmetic mean produces a value that is typical or representative of a given set of data. The algebraic formula for the arithmetic mean is:

$$F_t = (1/N)\sum X_t$$

where F_t = the forecast, N = number of observations and X_t = historic observations.

The examples described in this chapter can be found in the file **SMOOTH** on the CD accompanying this book. Each example has been placed on a separate worksheet.

Figure 3.1 takes the first set of data examined in Chapter 2 and gives examples of an estimation, the last observation and the arithmetic mean or average.

The AVERAGE function has been used to calculate the arithmetic mean.

HISTORIC MONTHLY SALES DATA FOR 1996/97

1996	JAN	FEB	MAR	APR	MAY	JUN	JUL	AUG	SEP	OCT	NOV	DEC
Sales Volume	63	57	59	48	55	61	61	45	54	68	56	66

1997	JAN	FEB	MAR	APR	MAY	JUN	JUL	AUG	SEP	OCT	NOV	DEC
Sales Volume	70	59	60	70	72	62	65	58	56	68	65	63

Estimation	75
Last observation	63
Arithmetic mean	61

Figure 3.1 Examples of an estimation, last observation and arithmetic mean

All three of the techniques shown in Figure 3.1 are regularly used in situations where there is little or no trend to influence the selection of a different forecasting approach. It is interesting to note the range of values that different individuals might choose to use for the forecast, ranging from as low as 61 to as high as 75.

The graph in Figure 3.2 shows the arithmetic mean plotted against the historic data. From this it can be seen that the arithmetic mean of 61 is a measure of central tendency, and there are approximately as many data points above as there are below the line.

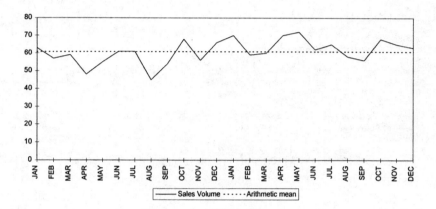

Figure 3.2 Arithmetic mean

MOVING AVERAGES

In an environment in which the data does not exhibit any significant trend and when using an average to calculate a future expected value, the earlier historic observations may have less relevance than the more recent observations, especially in cases where there is little evidence of trend or seasonality. In this case a *moving average* can be employed which allows early values to be dropped as later values are added. The algebraic formula for a moving average is as follows:

$$F_t = (1/N)\sum X_{t-i}$$

where F_t = the forecast, N = number of observations, X_t = historic observations and $_i$ = change in X_t variables.

The greater the value of N, the less the forecast will be affected by random fluctuations, or the greater the degree of *smoothing*. Furthermore, the greater the number of observations the slower the forecast is to respond to changes in the underlying pattern of the data. Figure 3.4 illustrates a three month moving average and a five month moving average and the results are shown graphically in Figure 3.5.

HISTORIC MONTHLY SALES DATA FOR 1996

1996	JAN	FEB	MAR	APR	MAY	JUN	JUL	AUG	SEP	OCT	NOV	DEC
Sales Volume	63	57	59	48	55	61	61	45	54	68	56	66
3 month moving average			59.67	54.67	54.00	54.67	59.00	55.67	53.33	55.67	59.33	63.33
5 month moving average					56.40	56.40	56.40	56.40	56.40	56.40	56.40	56.40

Figure 3.4 Three and five month moving averages

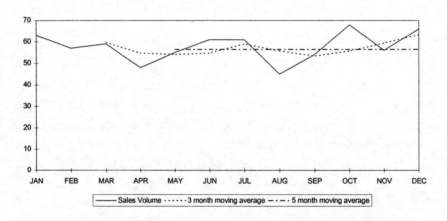

Figure 3.5 Graph showing three and five month moving averages

The three month moving average shown by the dotted line in Figure 3.5 quickly reflects changes in the data and is easily influenced by irregularities and fluctuations. The five month moving average shown by the dashed line, on the other hand, is very much smoother and shows very little influence of irregularities and fluctuations.

WEIGHTED MOVING AVERAGE

In addition to restricting the number of historic observations that are incorporated into a moving average, it is sometimes necessary to place more emphasis on some data points than on others. To this end a *weighted moving average* technique can be applied to the data. There are a number of different approaches to using weighted moving averages and the *proportional,* and *trend adjusted* methods are discussed here.

Proportional method

With the proportional method each value in the moving average is multiplied by a specified weight, and the total of the weights usually equals 1. The algebraic formula for this method is as follows:

$$F_t = P_1 X_1 + P_2 X_2 + ... + P_n X_n$$

where F_t = the forecast, X_t = historic observations and

$$P_1 + P_2 + ... Pn_1 = 1$$

Figure 3.6 shows the results of using the proportional method for calculating a three month weighted moving average compared to an unweighted three month moving average.

HISTORIC MONTHLY SALES DATA FOR 1996

1996	JAN	FEB	MAR	APR	MAY	JUN	JUL	AUG	SEP	OCT	NOV	DEC
Sales Volume	63	57	59	48	55	61	61	45	54	68	56	66
3 month moving average			59.67	54.67	54.00	54.67	59.00	55.67	53.33	55.67	59.33	63.33
3 month WMA (proportional)			59.20	53.10	53.70	56.60	59.80	53.00	52.70	59.20	59.20	63.40

Proportional weights	0.20	0.30	0.50

Figure 3.6 Three month moving average using the proportional method

The effect of the weights that have been used in the above example is to place a greater emphasis on the most recent historical observation. In other words the most recent occurrence is most important when determining the next occurrence. By looking at the actual value for the forecast period the weights could be changed in an attempt to produce a more accurate forecast for the next period.

Figure 3.7 shows the formula required for the weighted moving average and Figure 3.8 shows the unweighted and weighted moving averages plotted together on the same graph.

	A	B	C	D
1	HISTORIC MONTHLY SALES			
2				
3	1996	JAN	FEB	
4	Sales Volume	63	57	59
5				
6				
7	3 month moving average			=AVERAGE(B4:D4)
8	3 month WMA (proportional)			=AVERAGE(B4*$B$12+C4*$C$12+D4*$D$12)
9				
10				
11				
12	Proportional weights	0.2	0.3	0.5
13				

Figure 3.7 Formula required for weighted moving average

Note that the cell references to the proportional weights are absolute, i.e. $B$12, $C$12 and $D$12. This means that when the formula is copied the reference to cells B12, C12 and D12 remain fixed, whilst the other cell references are relative.

Trend adjusted method

If, as a result of examining the data, there is evidence of a trend, then a *trend adjusted* method of weighting the average can be applied. This involves assigning greater weights to more recent observations. There are a number of approaches to applying trend adjusted weights and the following is an example:

$$F_t = 2X_{t-1} - X_{t-2}$$

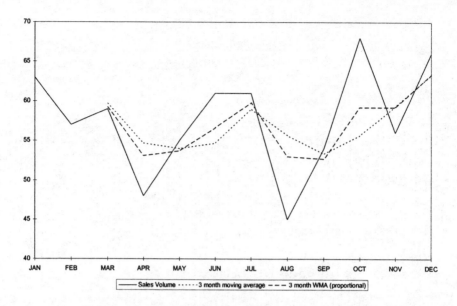

Figure 3.8 Graph showing unweighted and weighted
three month moving average

In this example the last observation is doubled before the observation before that is subtracted. This has the effect of using twice the increase in the value of the observations from period *t–2* to *t–1* in the forecast.

The effect of using this technique on the second set of data from Chapter 2 which showed some evidence of trend can be seen in Figure 3.9 and Figure 3.10 shows the results graphically.

	A	B	C	D	E	F	G	H	I	J	K	L	M
1	HISTORIC MONTHLY SALES DATA FOR 1996												
2	1996	JAN	FEB	MAR	APR	MAY	JUN	JUL	AUG	SEP	OCT	NOV	DEC
3	Sales Volume	25	28	30	35	31	33	40	35	33	35	35	43
4													
5	Trend adjusted moving average		31	32	40	27	35	47	30	31	37	35	51
6													

Figure 3.9 Trend adjusted moving average

The formula required in cell C5, which can be extrapolated for the remaining periods, is:

(C3*2)–B3

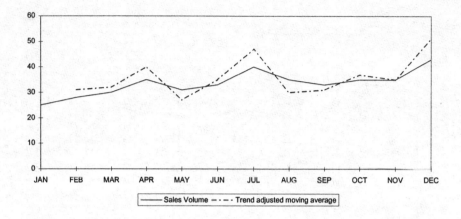

Figure 3.10 Trend adjusted moving average

ADAPTIVE FILTERING

Adaptive filtering is a technique used to re-evaluate the individual weights in a weighted average model to take into account the experience of actual results. Thus adaptive filtering allows a weighted average technique to learn from past errors and provides a systematic approach to adjusting the weights to the latest information available. The algebraic formula for adaptive filtering is as follows:

$$W'_t = W_t + 2K[(X_t - F_t) / X^2]X_{t-1}$$

where W'_t = the updated weight, W_t = the previous weight, X_t = the observation at time t, K = a constant, that is the training constant which may not be greater than $1/n$, and X = the largest of the most recent n values of X_t.

Figure 3.11 is a model for adaptive filtering.

	A	B	C	D	E
1	Weighted Moving Average with adaptive filtering				
2					
3			SALES FOR 1996		
4	QUARTER	1	2	3	4
5	ACTUAL SALES	12567	13456	9504	11000
6	OPEN WEIGHTS	0.20	0.20	0.20	0.40
7					
8			FORECAST FOR 1997		
9	QUARTER	5	6	7	8
10	FORECAST	11505	10198	0	0
11	ACTUAL SALES	11000	0	0	
12					
13	ADAPTIVE FILTERING - RECALCULATION OF NEW WEIGHTS				
14					
15	Adjusted weights for Qrt 6 forecast	0.18	0.18	0.17	0.38
16	Adjusted weights for Qrt 7 forecast	0.00	0.00	0.00	0.00
17	Adjusted weights for Qrt 8 forecast	0.00	0.00	0.00	0.00
18					
19					

Figure 3.11 Model for adaptive filtering

The plan consists of quarterly sales figures for 1996 and cell B10 is the initial forecast for the first quarter of 1997 which is calculated by multiplying the historic quarterly data by the opening proportional weights in row 6. Thus the formula for cell B10 is:

B5*B6+C5*C6+D5*D6+E5*E6

When the actual sales for the first quarter of 1997 become available the value is entered into cell B11. The adaptive filtering formula in cell B15 which is extrapolated into cells C15 through E15 calculates revised weights which are then referenced in cell C10 when the forecast for the second quarter of 1997 is calculated. The following is the formula entered into cell B15 and copied across to cell E15.

B6+2*0.25*(($B$11–$B$10)/$B$5^2)*B5

The forecast formula for the second quarter of 1997 in cell C10 is therefore:

C5*B15+D5*C15+E5*D15+B11*E15

It is not possible to copy the above formula as the references to the previous quarters are not in the same row and the revised weights for each quarter are also on different rows.

The adjusted weights will no longer total one because if the actual amount is less than the forecast then the combined weights will end up being less than one. The converse is true in that if the actual amount is more than the forecast the combined weights will total more than one.

In order to test the accuracy of the system enter an actual value that exactly matches the forecast. In this case the weights should not change, as no adjustment is required.

EXPONENTIAL SMOOTHING

Exponential smoothing is a weighted moving average technique which is especially effective when frequent re-forecasting is required, and when the forecasts must be achieved quickly. It is a short-term forecasting technique that is frequently used in the production and inventory environment, where only the next period's value is required to be forecast. Because only three numbers are required to perform exponential smoothing, this technique is simple to update. The data required are the historic observation, the latest data observation and the smoothing coefficient, or constant.

The smoothing coefficient α is a value between 0 and 1. A small value of, say, between 0.05 and 0.10 results in a high degree of smoothing and has the same effect as a large number of observations in a moving average calculation. A high coefficient value results in less smoothing and thus a high responsiveness to variations in the data. In the extreme, if the coefficient is 0 then the next period's forecast will be the same as the last period's forecast and if the coefficient is one, or unity, then the next period's forecast will be the same as the current period's data.

The primary assumption used in the simple form of this smoothing technique is that the data is stationary, i.e. that there is a clear trend present. Advanced exponential smoothing techniques are required if a trend or cycle is present in the data.

The algebraic formula for simple exponential smoothing is:

$$F_t = \alpha X_t + (1-\alpha)F_{t-1}$$

where $F_t{-}1$ = the previous forecast, X_t = the current observation and α = the smoothing coefficient. Figure 3.12 shows an example of exponential smoothing.

	A	B	C	D	E	F	G	H	I	J	K	L	M
1	Simple Exponential Smoothing												
2	HISTORIC MONTHLY SALES DATA FOR 1996												
3		JAN	FEB	MAR	APR	MAY	JUN	JUL	AUG	SEP	OCT	NOV	DEC
4	Sales Volume	114	121	119	120	115	125	119	120	128	119	122	118
5	E-S Coefficient	0.2											
6	Forecast	114	115	116	117	117	118	118	119	121	120	121	120
7													

Figure 3.12 Forecast using the exponential smoothing technique

The smoothing coefficient is first used in the second period of the forecast and the formula for cell C6 is:

C4*$B$5+(1–$B$5)*B6

With a low coefficient value of 0.20 a high degree of smoothing is expected and this is shown on the graph in Figure 3.13. Figure 3.14 shows the effect of a high smoothing coefficient where 0.80 has been entered into cell B5.

SUMMARY

There are many different approaches to averaging and smoothing as a means of forecasting. Moving averages and weighted moving averages are useful as a first step in forecasting, especially when there is no clear evidence of trend, seasonality or cycles. Adaptive filtering is very useful in a continuous forecasting situation where the actual data is available to assist in forecasting the next period.

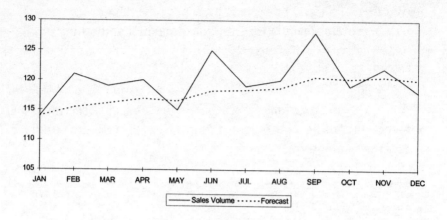

Figure 3.13 Forecast with a low coefficient of 0.20

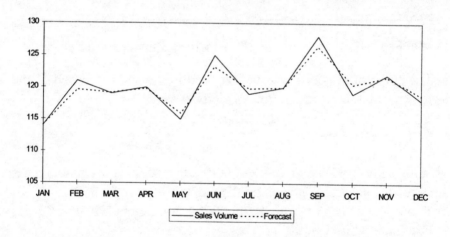

Figure 3.14 Forecast with a high coefficient of 0.80

Similarly, exponential smoothing does not require a great deal of historic data and is another useful tool for short-term forecasts.

None of the spreadsheet examples used in this chapter require the use of complicated spreadsheet functions and formulae. Indeed the AVERAGE function has been the main tool. However, the chapter has illustrated that having ascertained the algebraic formula for a particular technique it is not difficult to translate this into a formula that the spreadsheet understands. Once the formulae have been entered and tested the models can be used again and again with different data.

As with any forecasting technique it is important to always check what actually happened with the forecast data in order to ascertain how accurate the forecast was, and where necessary be able to adjust the forecast to better reflect the situation next time.

Regression Analysis

"One can't *believe impossible things,"* said *Alice.*
"I dare say you haven't had much practice," said the Queen. "When I
was your age, I always did it for half-an-hour a day. Why, sometimes
I've believed as many as six impossible things before breakfast."

Lewis Carroll, *Through the Looking Glass*, Ch. 5, first published in
1872, Chancellor Press, London, 1982.

INTRODUCTION

Many forecasting methods are based on the assumption that the
variable being forecast is related to something else. Thus sales
might vary according to the amount spent on advertising, or the life
of a component might be determined by how long it has been held
in the warehouse. Regression analysis is a widely used tool for
analysing the relationship between such variables and using these
variables for prediction purposes. For example, can variations in
the rate of interest be used to predict the amount of money
deposited in a building society?

To answer this question it is first important to establish that
there is indeed a relationship between the deposits in the building
society and interest rates. This is achieved by collecting a sample
data set of deposits and corresponding interest rates and then
plotting the data on a *scatter diagram*. A scatter diagram in this

case is an XY graph, which has been formatted to display only symbols, as opposed to a line.

From the sample data an equation can then be created that relates the two variables. This equation involves fitting a *least square line* to the data and is referred to as *simple linear regression*[1]. Simple here implies that only one variable is being used to predict another and is the converse to *multiple linear regression* which is discussed later in this chapter.

The algebraic formula for fitting a straight line is:

$$Y = MX + c$$

where Y = the independent variable, M = the slope or gradient of the line, (and is sometimes called the regression coefficient), X = the dependent variable and c is the constant, or intercept, sometimes referred to as the Y intercept. The c is the value of Y when X is zero. It is the base value of Y before any increase or decrease in X is taken into account. The independent variable (Y) is the variable to be predicted which in the above example would be the amounts deposited, and the dependent variable (X) is the variable used to do the predicting, which in this case is the interest rate.

In defining the least square line consider the annotated graph in Figure 4.1. For any given value of X there is a difference between $Y1$ and the value of Y determined by the line. The difference is denoted by D, which is referred to as a *deviation, residual,* or *error*. The least square line is defined as the line through a data set that has the property of minimising the sum of any given set of D^2s.

---

[1] The word 'regression' originates from the 19th century when Galton collected the heights of fathers and their sons and put forward the idea that, since very tall fathers tended to have slightly shorter sons, and very short fathers tended to have slightly taller sons, there would be what he termed a 'regression to the mean' (D. Rees,1991, Essential Statistics, Chapman and Hall).

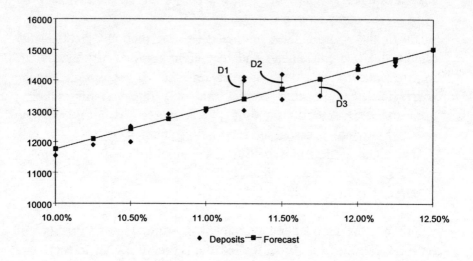

Figure 4.1 Least square line

Given the least square line approximation has the form $Y = MX + c$ this formula can be broken down as follows:

$$m = \frac{N\Sigma XY - (\Sigma X)(\Sigma Y)}{N\Sigma X^2 - (\Sigma X)^2}$$

and

$$c = \frac{(\Sigma Y)(\Sigma X)^2 - (\Sigma X)(\Sigma XY)}{N\Sigma X^2 - (\Sigma X)^2}$$

where N = the number of data points available, ΣX = the sum of the X data points, ΣY = the sum of the Y data points and ΣXY = the sum of the product of each set of data.

Having established the equation representing the least square line, an estimate of a value for Y corresponding to a value for X may be obtained. When the least square line is being used in this way it has a *regression line* of Y on X, since Y is estimated from a value of X.

PREPARING THE DATA

Figure 4.2 is a sample of amounts deposited into a building society and corresponding interest rates. The data has been sorted by the independent variable, i.e. the interest rates. This example and the others in this chapter can be found on the CD accompanying this book under the filename **REGRESS**.

The first step is to create an XY graph, formatted as a scatter diagram to establish whether there is sufficient relationship between the two variables to be able to calculate a linear regression line that will be worth while. This is shown in Figure 4.3.

	A	B	C
1	Simple linear regression		
2	INTEREST RATES AND CASH DEPOSITS		
3	(Independent - X)	(Dependent - Y)	
4	Interest rates	Deposits	
5	10.00%	11550	
6	10.25%	11900	
7	10.50%	12500	
8	10.50%	11990	
9	10.75%	12900	
10	11.00%	13000	
11	11.25%	14000	
12	11.25%	13020	
13	11.25%	14000	
14	11.25%	14100	
15	11.50%	13380	
16	11.50%	14200	
17	11.75%	13500	
18	11.75%	14050	
19	12.00%	14500	
20	12.00%	14100	
21	12.25%	14500	
22	12.25%	14600	
23	12.50%	15000	

Figure 4.2 Data for regression analysis

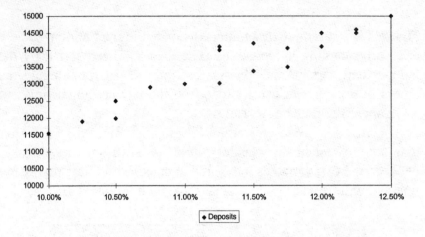

Figure 4.3 Scatter diagram of data showing a strong correlation

The graph in Figure 4.3 clearly indicates a relationship between the two variables. Had this not been the case the points on the graph would be scattered more widely. Figure 4.4 is scatter diagram showing the number of aircraft sold at different rainfall levels and it is clear from this graph that there is no relationship between these two variables, as one would of course expect.

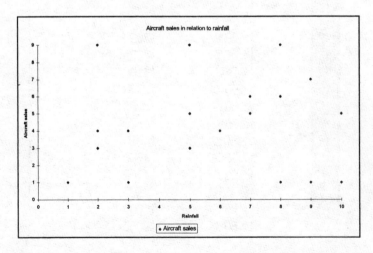

Figure 4.4 Scatter diagram showing no discernible relationship between the variables

CALCULATING THE LEAST SQUARE LINE

The least square line can be calculated either through the use of the Regression command or by using the FORECAST function in Excel and the REGRESSION function in 1-2-3.

The function approach

The FORECAST and REGRESSION functions work in different ways and are therefore explained separately in the sections that follow.

The Excel FORECAST function

Figure 4.5 shows the results of the Excel FORECAST function. The following formula was entered into cell D5.

```
=FORECAST(A5,$B$5:$B$23,$A$5:$A$23)
```

Note in the above formula that it is important to reference the range for the dependent variable first, followed by the range for the independent variable. These references are absolute in order that they remain fixed when the formula is extrapolated for the remaining cells in the range.

The data in column E can now be plotted as a line onto the scatter diagram. A simple way to do this in Excel is to select the range, Copy it to the Clipboard, access and select the chart and then select Paste. Figure 4.6 shows the forecast line on the scatter diagram.

The regression line and regression equation applies only within the range of the independent or X range of data. The line should not be extrapolated much below the minimum value of X or above the maximum value of X. Similarly the regression equation should not be used for values of X outside the range of data.

	A	B	C	D
1	Regression Analysis using Standard Formulae.			
2	INTEREST RATES AND CASH DEPOSITS			
3	(Independent - X)	(Dependent - Y)		
4	Interest rates	Deposits		Forecast
5	10.00%	11550		11768.09
6	10.25%	11900		12093.55
7	10.50%	12500		12419.00
8	10.50%	11990		12419.00
9	10.75%	12900		12744.45
10	11.00%	13000		13069.91
11	11.25%	14000		13395.36
12	11.25%	13020		13395.36
13	11.25%	14000		13395.36
14	11.25%	14100		13395.36
15	11.50%	13380		13720.81
16	11.50%	14200		13720.81
17	11.75%	13500		14046.27
18	11.75%	14050		14046.27
19	12.00%	14500		14371.72
20	12.00%	14100		14371.72
21	12.25%	14500		14697.17
22	12.25%	14600		14697.17
23	12.50%	15000		15022.62

Figure 4.5 Calculated straight line using the Excel FORECAST function

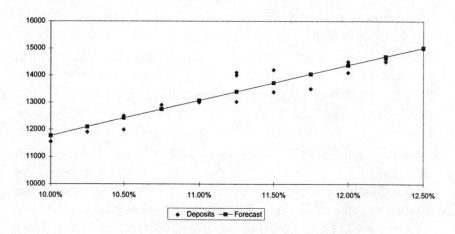

Figure 4.6 Scatter diagram with regression line

Two other Excel functions that are useful in this context are
INTERCEPT and SLOPE which calculate the values for c and M

respectively in the formula $Y = MX + c$. Figure 4.7 shows the results of these functions. The following formulae were entered into cells E5 and F5 respectively:

=INTERCEPT(B5:B23,A5:A23)
=SLOPE(B5:B23,A5:A23)

The results of these two functions can be used to calculate the forecast which is useful as an auditing tool to cross-check the result produced using the FORECAST function. The following formula is required in cell G5:

=$F$5*A5+$E$5

	A	B	C	D	E	F	G
2	INTEREST RATES AND CASH DEPOSITS						
3	(Independent - X)	(Dependent - Y)					
4	Interest rates	Deposits		Forecast	Intercept	Slope	Forecast
5	10.00%	11550		11768.09	-1250.02	130181.2	11768.09
6	10.25%	11900		12093.55			
7	10.50%	12500		12419.00			
8	10.50%	11990		12419.00			
9	10.75%	12900		12744.45			
10	11.00%	13000		13069.91			
11	11.25%	14000		13395.36			
12	11.25%	13020		13395.36			
13	11.25%	14000		13395.36			
14	11.25%	14100		13395.36			
15	11.50%	13380		13720.81			
16	11.50%	14200		13720.81			
17	11.75%	13500		14046.27			
18	11.75%	14050		14046.27			
19	12.00%	14500		14371.72			
20	12.00%	14100		14371.72			
21	12.25%	14500		14697.17			
22	12.25%	14600		14697.17			
23	12.50%	15000		15022.62			

Figure 4.7 Results of Excel INTERCEPT and SLOPE functions

The 1-2-3 REGRESSION function

The REGRESSION function in 1-2-3 requires the X and Y variables to be specified followed by a choice of results to be returned based on the selection of a numeric attribute. The options are:

1	Constant;
2	Standard error of Y estimate;
3	R squared;
4	Number of observations;
5	Degrees of freedom;
101	X coefficient (slope) for the independent variable specified by attribute;
201	Standard error of coefficient for the independent variable specified by attribute.

Therefore to calculate the Constant for the example in Figure 4.8 the following formula is required in cell F4:

@REGRESSION($A$5..$A$23,$B$5..$B$23,1)

and to calculate the slope, or X coefficient the formula in cell F5 is:

@REGRESSION($A$5..$A$23,$B$5..$B$23,101)

The results of these two formulae can then be used to calculate the forecast with the following formula in cell C5, which can be extrapolated for all the variables.

+$F$5*A5+$F$4

Figure 4.8 shows the 1-2-3 REGRESSION function being applied.

The command approach

Both Excel and 1-2-3 have a command option for regression analysis.

	A	B	C	D	E	F	G	H	I
1	Regression Analysis using Standard Formulae.								
2	INTEREST RATES AND CASH DEPOSITS								
3	(Independent-X)	(Dependent-Y)							
4	Interest rates	Deposits	Forecast	Constant	@REGRESSION($A$5..$A$23,$B$5..$B$23,1)				
5	10.00%	11550	+$F$5*A5+$F$4	X Coefficient	@REGRESSION($A$5..$A$23,$B$5..$B$23,101)				
6	10.25%	11900	+$F$5*A6+$F$4						
7	10.50%	12500	+$F$5*A7+$F$4						
8	10.50%	11990	+$F$5*A8+$F$4						
9	10.75%	12900	+$F$5*A9+$F$4						
10	11.00%	13000	+$F$5*A10+$F$4						
11	11.25%	14000	+$F$5*A11+$F$4						
12	11.25%	13020	+$F$5*A12+$F$4						
13	11.25%	14000	+$F$5*A13+$F$4						
14	11.25%	14100	+$F$5*A14+$F$4						
15	11.50%	13380	+$F$5*A15+$F$4						
16	11.50%	14200	+$F$5*A16+$F$4						
17	11.75%	13500	+$F$5*A17+$F$4						
18	11.75%	14050	+$F$5*A18+$F$4						
19	12.00%	14500	+$F$5*A19+$F$4						
20	12.00%	14100	+$F$5*A20+$F$4						
21	12.25%	14500	+$F$5*A21+$F$4						
22	12.25%	14600	+$F$5*A22+$F$4						
23	12.50%	15000	+$F$5*A23+$F$4						
24									

Figure 4.8 Using the 1-2-3 REGRESSION function

The 1-2-3 regression command

The Range Analyse Regression command in 1-2-3 calculates a number of statistics, including the slope and the intercept, which are used to produce the formula for the regression line.

The command requires a range for the independent, or X variable and a range for the dependent, or Y variable, to be specified together with an output range, which specifies where the results of the command will be placed. Figure 4.9 shows a completed dialogue box and Figure 4.10 shows the results of the 1-2-3 Regression command.

In order to calculate the regression line the following formula is required in cell C5, which can then be extrapolated for the remaining variables:

+$G$11*A5+$H$5

Note that the references to cell G11, the slope or X coefficient and cell H5, the constant or intercept, are absolute references in order that they remain fixed when the formula is extrapolated.

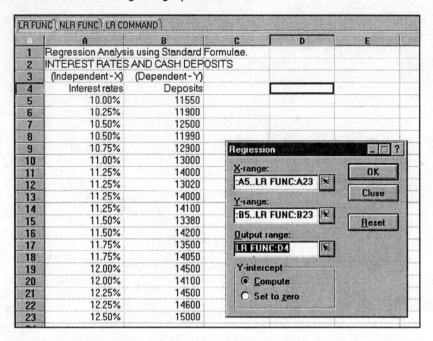

Figure 4.9 1-2-3 Regression command dialogue box

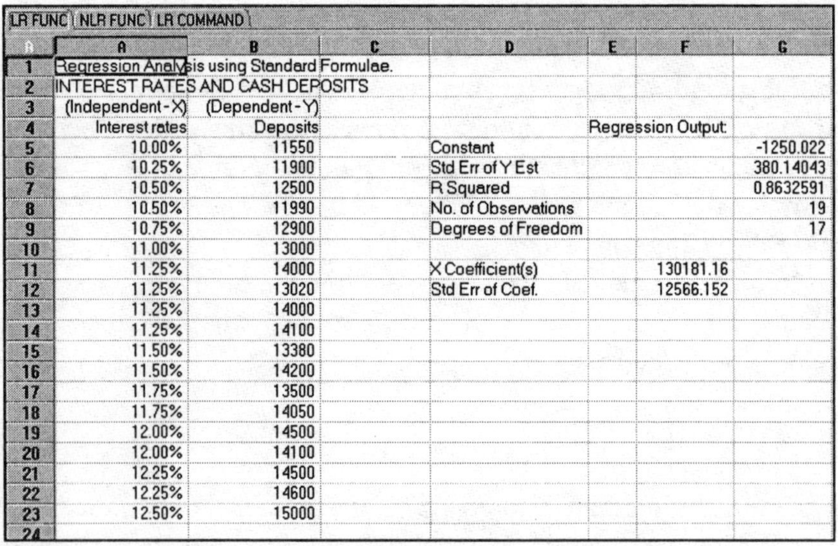

Figure 4.10 Results of the 1-2-3 Regression command

Figure 4.11 shows the forecast results. The forecast data can then be plotted on the scatter diagram as already explained.

	A	B	C	D	E	F	G	H
	LR FUNC	NLR FUNC	LR COMMAND					
1	Regression Analysis using Standard Formulae.							
2	INTEREST RATES AND CASH DEPOSITS							
3	(Independent - X)	(Dependent - Y)						
4	Interest rates	Deposits	Forecast		Regression Output			
5	10.00%	11550	11768.09		Constant			-1250.0216
6	10.25%	11900	12093.55		Std Err of Y Est			380.140431
7	10.50%	12500	12419.00		R Squared			0.86325912
8	10.50%	11990	12419.00		No. of Observations			19
9	10.75%	12900	12744.45		Degrees of Freedom			17
10	11.00%	13000	13069.91					
11	11.25%	14000	13395.36		X Coefficient(s)	130181.16		
12	11.25%	13020	13395.36		Std Err of Coef.	12566.152		
13	11.25%	14000	13395.36					
14	11.25%	14100	13395.36					
15	11.50%	13380	13720.81					
16	11.50%	14200	13720.81					
17	11.75%	13500	14046.27					
18	11.75%	14050	14046.27					
19	12.00%	14500	14371.72					
20	12.00%	14100	14371.72					
21	12.25%	14500	14697.17					
22	12.25%	14600	14697.17					
23	12.50%	15000	15022.62					
24								

Figure 4.11 Results of applying the 1-2-3 Regression command

The Excel Regression command

To use the Regression command in Excel it is necessary to have the Analysis Toolpak[2] installed and enabled. Once enabled Data Analysis becomes the last option on the Tools menu and within Data Analysis one of the options is Regression. The command requires the same information as 1-2-3, i.e. references to the X and Y data and a location for the output. Figure 4.12 shows the results of the command where the output range was selected as a new worksheet.

---

[2] The Analysis Toolpak is a standard part of the Excel package, but if a custom installation was selected during Setup it is possible that this option was not selected. Refer to your Excel manual for further information on installation.

	A	B	C	D	E	F	G	H	I
1	SUMMARY OUTPUT								
2									
3	*Regression Statistics*								
4	Multiple R	0.93							
5	R Square	0.86							
6	Adjusted R Square	0.86							
7	Standard Error	380.14							
8	Observations	19.00							
9									
10	ANOVA								
11		*df*	*SS*	*MS*	*F*	*Significance F*			
12	Regression	1.00	15508858.98	15508858.98	107.32	0.00			
13	Residual	17.00	2456614.70	144506.75					
14	Total	18.00	17965473.68						
15									
16		*Coefficients*	*Standard Error*	*t Stat*	*P-value*	*Lower 95%*	*Upper 95%*	*Lower 95.0%*	*Upper 95.0%*
17	Intercept	-1250.02	1427.93	-0.88	0.39	-4262.70	1762.66	-4262.70	1762.66
18	Interest rates	130181.16	12566.15	10.36	0.00	103668.87	156693.46	103668.87	156693.46
19									

Figure 4.12 Results of Excel Regression command

The regression formula can be created in the same way as shown for 1-2-3 by referencing the intercept or constant in cell B17 and the X coefficient in cell B18.

FUNCTION VS. COMMAND

The previous section has explained how to perform regression analysis using spreadsheet functions and spreadsheet commands. It is generally preferable to apply functions as opposed to commands wherever possible. This is because functions are dynamic formulae that are recalculated when anything in the spreadsheet changes. Therefore having set up a model such as the one used in this chapter, a different set of sample data could be entered into columns A and B and all the regression formulae and the chart will automatically reflect the changed data. This is not the case with a command, because on executing the command only the resulting values are placed in the spreadsheet without the underlying formula. Therefore to recalculate after making a change it is necessary to execute the Regression command again.

THE GRAPHIC APPROACH WITH EXCEL

Excel has the ability to plot a trend line onto a graph without having to calculate the equation beforehand. Figure 4.13 shows the original scatter diagram on which the data series has been selected and the command Insert Trendline has been taken.

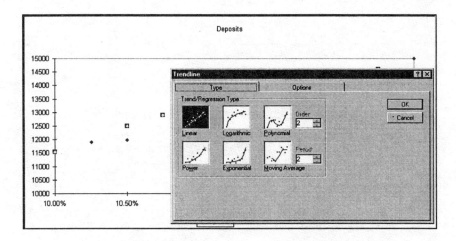

Figure 4.13 Inserting a trendline onto an Excel chart

The first option is most suitable for this example, but non-linear trendlines can also be inserted if appropriate. Figure 4.14 shows the resulting trendline. Although the individual calculations behind the line cannot be seen, selecting Format Trendline Options allows the formula to be displayed as shown in Figure 4.14.

STANDARD ERROR

An additional refinement of linear regression is to incorporate the *standard error* of the estimate. The standard error has many of the properties analogous to the standard deviation.

For example, if lines are drawn on either side of the regression line of Y on X at respective vertical distances, confidence limits may be established.

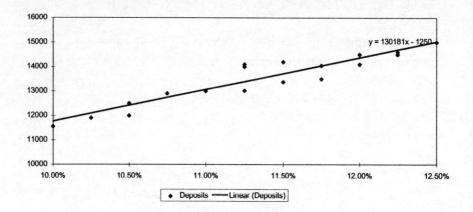

Figure 4.14 Trendline inserted onto an Excel chart

The algebraic formula for a 95% confidence limit is

$$(a + bx_0) \pm ts_r \sqrt{\left[\frac{1}{n} + \frac{(x_0 - \bar{x})^2}{\sum x^2 - \frac{(\sum x)^2}{n}}\right]}$$

Figure 4.15 shows the results of calculating upper and lower confidence limits. Two columns have been inserted into the original spreadsheet so that the already calculated forecast is in column E and the lower and upper standard errors will be placed in columns C and D respectively. The formula required in cell C5 to calculate the lower confidence limit is as follows:

In Excel:

```
=E5–'LR Command'!$D$18*'LR Command'!$B$7*SQRT
   (1+1/'LR Command'!$B$8+(A5–AVERAGE($A$5:$A$23)^2/
      'LR Command'!$B$8*STDEV($A$5:$A$23)))
```

The regression command output in Figure 4.12 has been placed on a sheet called *LR Command* and this is seen in the formula when referencing the Student *t* distribution, the standard error and the number of observations.

In 1-2-3:

```
+E5–10.36*$J$6*@SQRT(1+1/$J$8+(A5–@AVG($A$5..$A$23)^2/
  $J$6*@STD($A$5..$A$23)))
```

The above 1-2-3 formula has been entered in cell C5 of the spreadsheet in Figure 4.11, after inserting two columns for the lower and upper standard errors. The Student *t* distribution is entered as a value as the Regression command does not supply it.

To calculate the upper confidence limit in cell D5 only the beginning of the formula is different to the lower confidence limit. In this case the formula begins with E5+ ...

The results of these formulae are shown in Figure 4.15 and Figure 4.16 shows the lines plotted onto the graph.

	A	B	C	D	E
1	Regression Analysis using Standard Formulae.				
2	INTEREST RATES AND CASH DEPOSITS				
3	(Independent - X)	(Dependent - Y)		Standard error	
4	Interest rates	Deposits	Lower limit	Upper limit	Forecast
5	10.00%	11550	7540.10	15996.09	11768.09
6	10.25%	11900	7860.97	16326.12	12093.55
7	10.50%	12500	8181.85	16656.15	12419.00
8	10.50%	11990	8181.85	16656.15	12419.00
9	10.75%	12900	8502.73	16986.18	12744.45
10	11.00%	13000	8823.61	17316.20	13069.91
11	11.25%	14000	9144.50	17646.22	13395.36
12	11.25%	13020	9144.50	17646.22	13395.36
13	11.25%	14000	9144.50	17646.22	13395.36
14	11.25%	14100	9144.50	17646.22	13395.36
15	11.50%	13380	9465.40	17976.23	13720.81
16	11.50%	14200	9465.40	17976.23	13720.81
17	11.75%	13500	9786.30	18306.23	14046.27
18	11.75%	14050	9786.30	18306.23	14046.27
19	12.00%	14500	10107.20	18636.23	14371.72
20	12.00%	14100	10107.20	18636.23	14371.72
21	12.25%	14500	10428.11	18966.23	14697.17
22	12.25%	14600	10428.11	18966.23	14697.17
23	12.50%	15000	10749.03	19296.22	15022.62

Figure 4.15 Results of standard error calculations

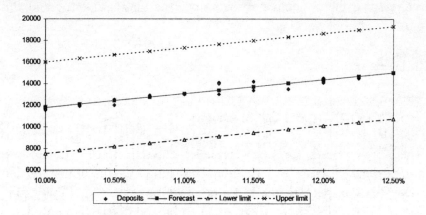

Figure 4.16 Regression line with upper and lower confidence limits

MULTIPLE LINEAR REGRESSION

When two or more dependent (*X*) variables are required for a prediction the analysis is referred to as *multiple linear regression*.

The simple linear regression equation can be adapted to accommodate multiple dependent variables in the following way:

$$Y = A_0 + A_1 X_1 + A_2 X_2 + \ldots + A_n X_n$$

Theoretically there is no limit to the number of independent variables that can be analysed, but within the spreadsheet the maximum is 75. This is a far greater number than would ever actually be required in a business situation.

The following example in Figure 4.17 represents expenditure on advertising and sales promotion together with sales achieved, where the advertising and sales promotion are dependent variables and the sales achieved is the independent variable. The requirement is to estimate future sales by entering advertising and promotion expenditure and applying the multiple regression equation to predict the sales value.

	A	B	C	D	E	F	G
1	Dependent - X1	Dependent - X2	Independent - Y				
2	Advertising	Sales Promotion	Sales				
3	123	63	900		Estimation of future sales volumes		
4	234	117	1000				
5	321	161	1200		Estimated sales		
6	234	117	1050		Advertising expenditure		
7	231	116	876		Promotion Expenditure		
8	234	117	778				
9	432	216	1550				
10	234	117	777				
11	333	167	678				
12	234	117	876				

Figure 4.17 Multiple regression scenario

Multiple linear regression with Excel

In Excel there are no built-in functions for multiple regression and therefore the command method is required. Figure 4.18 shows the results of the Excel Regression command where the range C3:C12 from Figure 4.17 was specified as the independent variable and A3:B12 from Figure 4.17 as the dependent variables. The regression output has been placed on the same sheet commencing in cell A14.

In order to calculate the estimated sales value in cell G5 the data in cells B30, B31 and B32 shown in Figure 4.18 are required and the formula for cell G5 is:

(G6*B31)+(G7*B32)+B30

To use this multiple regression model data must first be entered into cells G6 and G7. Figure 4.19 shows the estimated sales value if the advertising expenditure is 250 and the promotion expenditure is 125.

	A	B	C	D	E	F	G	H	I
14	SUMMARY OUTPUT								
15									
16	Regression Statistics								
17	Multiple R	0.616175498							
18	R Square	0.379672245							
19	Adjusted R Squ	0.202435743							
20	Standard Error	226.4243946							
21	Observations	10							
22									
23	ANOVA								
24		df	SS	MS	F	Significance F			
25	Regression	2	219650.4548	109825.2	2.142179	0.1880071			
26	Residual	7	358876.0452	51268.01					
27	Total	9	578526.5						
28									
29		Coefficients	Standard Error	t Stat	P-value	Lower 95%	Upper 95%	Lower 95.0%	Upper 95.0%
30	Intercept	421.2665987	299.2793684	1.407603	0.20207	-286.41615	1128.949	-286.416	1128.949
31	Advertising	-30.5718863	86.26753425	-0.35438	0.733486	-234.56204	173.4183	-234.562	173.4183
32	Sales Promotion	65.18727619	173.4035007	0.375928	0.718104	-344.84655	475.2211	-344.847	475.2211
33									

Figure 4.18 Results of Excel Regression command for multiple linear regression

Providing the X and Y data does not change, different values can be entered into cells G6 and G7 and the estimated sales value will recalculate correctly. However, because the command method has been used for the regression, if any of the X or Y data changes it will be necessary to execute the Regression command again.

	A	B	C	D	E	F	G
1	Dependent - X1	Dependent - X2	Independent - Y				
2	Advertising	Sales Promotion	Sales				
3	123	63	900		Estimation of future sales volumes		
4	234	117	1000				
5	321	161	1200		Estimated sales		927
6	234	117	1050		Advertising expenditure		250
7	231	116	876		Promotion Expenditure		125
8	234	117	778				
9	432	216	1550				
10	234	117	777				
11	333	167	678				
12	234	117	876				

Figure 4.19 Results of multiple regression using the Excel command method

Multiple linear regression with 1-2-3

In 1-2-3 the regression command can be used for multiple regression in much the same way as shown above in Excel. However it is also possible to use the REGRESSION function which is illustrated in Figure 4.20. The following formulae are required in cells F9, F10 and F11 respectively:

@REGRESSION(A3..B12,C3..C12,1)
@REGRESSION(A3..B12,C3..C12,101)
@REGRESSION(A3..B12,C3..C12,102)

As already mentioned the spreadsheets allow up to 75 independent variables to be specified and in the above formulae this is reflected with the attribute numbers 101 and 102 which can go up to 175 as necessary.

	A	B	C	D	E	F	G
1	Dependent-X1	Dependent-X2	Independent-Y				
2	Advertising	Promotion	Sales				
3	123	63	900		Estimation of future sales volumes		
4	234	117	1000				
5	321	161	1200		Estimated sales		927
6	234	117	1050		Advertising expenditure		250
7	231	116	876		Promotion Expenditure		125
8	234	117	778				
9	432	216	1550		Constant	421.266599	
10	234	117	777		Advertising	-30.571886	
11	333	167	678		Promotion	65.1872762	
12	234	117	876				

Figure 4.20 Results of multiple regression using the
1-2-3 REGRESSION function

The results of these formulae are referenced in cell G5 to calculate the estimated sales as follows:

+(G6*F10)+(G7*F11)+F9

Selecting variables for multiple regression

A problem encountered when applying multiple regression methods in forecasting is deciding which variables to use. In the interests of obtaining as accurate a forecast as possible it is obvious that all the relevant variables should be included. However, it is often not feasible to do this, because, apart from the complexity of the resulting equation, the following factors must be considered.

1. In a forecasting situation the inclusion of variables which do not significantly contribute to the regression merely inflate the error of the resulting prediction.
2. The cost of monitoring many variables may be very high – so it is advisable to exclude variables that are not contributing significantly.
3. There is no point including terms that contribute less than the error variance, unless there is strong prior evidence that a particular variable should be included.
4. For successful forecasting, an equation that is stable over a wide range of conditions is necessary. The smaller the number of variables in the equation, the more stable and reliable the equation.

SUMMARY

Regression analysis is a popular forecasting and estimating technique. Although many users might find the mathematics involved quite difficult, the technique itself is relatively easy to use, especially when a model or template has previously been developed.

However, users who do not understand the underlying mathematics should obtain some assistance in the interpretation of the results.

5

Time Series Analysis

Technology is the acknowledged master, the engine that pulls all the rest along and determines where the future shall be, how fast it shall be attained, what we shall do within it, and who shall prosper, who shall languish, who shall fossilize.

T. Levitt, *Marketing in an Electronic Age*, Edited by R. Buzzell, Harvard Business School, Research Colloquium, 1985.

INTRODUCTION

A time series is a set of observations recorded over a time period. It is a sequence of data that is usually observed at equal intervals.

Time series analysis predicts the value of an item by studying the past movements of that item. It is a series that uses time as the independent or explanatory variable.

Time series data are analysed for *trend*, *seasonal fluctuations*, and *residual*. Trend analysis involves using a linear regression model with time as the independent variable. The data is also adjusted for seasonal fluctuations since this can significantly influence the regression results. The residual is what is left over after the trend and seasonality has been taken into account, and in this case consists of a *cycle* and an *error*.

Many time series follow a cycle, with either an annual or seasonal pattern. These cyclical effects are analysed, as are the errors. This is achieved through *decomposition* analysis.

Decomposition analysis is the method of reducing a set of time series data to a trend, a seasonal factor and a residual. This may be expressed as:

$$D=T\,S\,R$$

where D = data, T = trend, S = seasonality factor and R = residual which includes the error.

The decomposition analysis may be either multiplicative or additive. Additive decomposition takes the following form:

$$D=T+S+R$$

and multiplicative decomposition analysis takes the form:

$$D=T*S*R$$

The multiplicative model is also referred to as a *ration model*. It is the multiplicative model that is used in this chapter.

MULTIPLICATIVE TIME SERIES ANALYSIS

The decomposition method described here fits a linear regression line to a set of historic quarterly sales data, establishes the trend, and then uses a centred weighted moving average to isolate the seasonality. The residual from the difference between the data trend and the seasonality is then deduced.

The cyclical component of a series may be estimated by comparing the actual value for each month, with the centred moving average for the month. Since the centred moving average is based on four quarters and is equally weighted with data from before and after the periods in question the moving average should be free of seasonal effects and should not be affected by trend.

The de-seasonalised series consists of the historic series, but with the seasonal fluctuations removed. It is a useful aid for judging the overall behaviour of the historic series because the distraction of the seasonal fluctuations has been removed. It is also useful for judging whether one or more values in the historic series deviate appreciably from the general trend. It is important to detect, and if possible explain such anomalies in order to anticipate potential future recurrences.

The trend describes the long-term behaviour of the series after the removal of the seasonal effects and the irregularities due to short-term random fluctuations. The trend is shown by means of a straight line whose slope indicates the long-term increase or decrease per unit time in the series.

The seasonal component indicates the adjustments that act on the trend due to seasonality. These are expressed as percentages, and repeat themselves in each year.

The residuals are also expressed as percentages. They represent the deviations from the combined series consisting of trend and seasonal components. Allowances are made for the possibility that the residuals may exhibit cyclical behaviour.

A TIME SERIES ANALYSIS MODEL

The development of a time series model requires a moderate amount of statistical knowledge that is beyond the scope of this book to explain in detail. However the system shown in this chapter is a good example of how a complex application can be developed in such a way that it can be used by less experienced people to great effect. The template on the CD accompanying this book which is called **TIMESERA** can be used without amendment to produce quarterly time series forecasts and readers wishing to examine the theory behind the formulae can study the *Calculation and Processing* worksheet.

The approach to developing the quarterly time series forecasting system is described in this chapter and the model consists of three worksheets which have been called *Data Input and Output, Calculation and Processing*, and *Graphics*.

Data input and output

The *Data Input and Output* sheet consists of an input form that captures the historic data. The model has been designed to collect historic quarterly data for a three year period. On the same sheet the final results of the time series analysis are displayed in order that comparisons can be made with the historic data.

Figure 5.1 shows the completed *Data Input and Output* sheet together with some sample data.

	A	B	C	D	E
1	TIME SERIES MULTIPLICATIVE MODEL FOR QUARTERLY DATA				
2					
3	3 YEARS HISTORIC DATA IS REQUIRED TO PRODUCE A FORECAST				
4		Qrt-1	Qrt-2	Qrt-3	Qrt-4
5	Earliest year (T-3)	6500	6950	7200	8500
6	Year after (T-2)	6900	7200	7500	7700
7	Last Year (T-1)	7300	7600	8200	9000
8					
9	RESULTS OF TIME SERIES ANALYSIS				
10		Qrt-1	Qrt-2	Qrt-3	Qrt-4
11	Forecast for T+1	7955.53	8286.13	8684.79	9602.52
12	Forecast for T+2	8424.91	8804.65	9219.89	10185.19
13	Forecast for T+3	8928.49	9323.18	9754.99	10767.85
14					

Figure 5.1 Input and Output worksheet with data

Cells B11 through E13 contain references to cells in the *Calculation and Processing* sheet as no calculations are performed on the *Data Input and Output* sheet. This can be seen in Figure 5.2

	A	B	C	D
1	TIME SERIES MU			
2				
3	3 YEARS HISTOR			
4		Qrt-1	Qrt-2	Qrt-3
5	Earliest year (T-3)	6500	6950	7200
6	Year after (T-2)	6900	7200	7500
7	Last Year (T-1)	7300	7600	8200
8				
9	RESULTS OF TIM			
10		Qrt-1	Qrt-2	Qrt-3
11	Forecast for T+1	='Calculation and Processing'!B21	='Calculation and Processing'!C21	='Calculation and Processing'!D21
12	Forecast for T+2	='Calculation and Processing'!F21	='Calculation and Processing'!G21	='Calculation and Processing'!H21
13	Forecast for T+3	='Calculation and Processing'!J21	='Calculation and Processing'!K21	='Calculation and Processing'!L21

Figure 5.2 Cell contents for Input and Output worksheet

Calculation and processing

The *Calculation and Processing* sheet contains the formulae for decomposing the historic data to establish the trend, seasonality and residual and then to provide the forecast data with standard deviations. Figures 5.3 and 5.4 show the results section of the *Calculation and Processing* sheet and Figures 5.5 and 5.6 show the work area required to calculate some of the statistics for which there are no built-in statistical functions.

	A	B	C	D	E	F	G
1	CALCULATION AND PROCESSING FOR TIME SERIES ANALYSIS						
2		1	2	3	4	5	6
3	12 periods of quarterly data	Q1	Q2	Q3	Q4	Q5	Q6
4	Historic data	6500	6950	7200	8500	6900	7200
5							
6	Trend	6810.26	6944.00	7077.74	7211.48	7345.22	7478.96
7	Seasonal Components	94.1%	96.9%	100.0%	108.9%	94.1%	96.9%
8	Residual	101.4%	103.3%	101.7%	108.2%	99.8%	99.3%
9	Seasonally adjusted data	6905.20	7170.39	7198.21	7804.12	7330.14	7428.32
10	Trend and seasonally adjusted	6410.62	6730.57	7079.50	7854.52	6914.20	7249.09
11							
12	Forecast period number	13	14	15	16	17	18
13	Forecast quarters	Q13	Q14	Q15	Q16	Q17	Q18
14	Forecast Trend Values	8415.15	8548.89	8682.63	8816.38	8950.12	9083.86
15	Seasonal components	94.1%	96.9%	100.0%	108.9%	94.1%	96.9%
16	Residual components	1.0043	1.0000	1.0000	1.0000	1.0000	1.0000
17		'					
18	FORECASTS	Q13	Q14	Q15	Q16	Q17	Q18
19	Very Low (-4 STD)	4679.91	5010.51	5409.17	6326.90	5149.29	5529.03
20	Low (-2STD)	6317.72	6648.32	7046.98	7964.71	6787.10	7166.84
21	Mean	7955.53	8286.13	8684.79	9602.52	8424.91	8804.65
22	High (+ 2STD)	9593.34	9923.94	10322.60	11240.33	10062.72	10442.46
23	Very High (+4 STD)	11231.15	11561.75	11960.41	12878.14	11700.53	12080.27

Figure 5.3 Results section of calculation and processing worksheet

Rows 6 to 10 of the *Calculation and Processing* sheet decompose the historical data to show the trend, the seasonal components and the residual.

The trend describes the long-term behaviour of the series after removal of the seasonal effects and the irregularities due to short-term random fluctuations. It is described by means of a straight line, the slope of which indicates the long-term rate of increase or decrease per unit time in the series. The trend is computed using the centred moving average calculated in row 28 which has the effect of smoothing out seasonal fluctuations and (to some degree) short-term irregularities.

	A	B	C
1	CALCULATION AND PROCESS		
2		1	=B2+1
3	12 periods of quarterly data	Q1	Q2
4	Historic data	='Input and Output'!B5	='Input and Output'!C5
5			
6	Trend	=FORECAST(B2,$B$4:$M$4,$B$2:$M$2)	=FORECAST(C2,$B$4:$M$4,$B$2:$M$2)
7	Seasonal Components	=$B$32/$B$31	=$C$32/$B$31
8	Residual	=B33	=C33
9	Seasonally adjusted data	=B4/B7	=C4/C7
10	Trend and seasonally adjusted	=B6*B7	=C6*C7
11			
12	Forecast period number	13	=B12+1
13	Forecast quarters	Q13	Q14
14	Forecast Trend Values	=FORECAST(B12,$B$4:$M$4,$B$2:$M$2)	=FORECAST(C12,$B$4:$M$4,$B$2:$M$2)
15	Seasonal components	=$B$32/$B$31	=$C$32/$B$31
16	Residual components	=B34*B39+1	=C34*C39+1
17			
18	FORECASTS	Q13	Q14
19	Very Low (-4 STD)	=B21-4*STDEVA($B$21:$M$21)	=C21-4*STDEVA($B$21:$M$21)
20	Low (-2STD)	=B21-2*STDEVA($B$21:$M$21)	=C21-2*STDEVA($B$21:$M$21)
21	Mean	=B14*B15*B16	=C14*C15*C16
22	High (+ 2STD)	=B21+2*STDEVA($B$21:$M$21)	=C21+2*STDEVA($B$21:$M$21)
23	Very High (+4 STD)	=B21+4*STDEVA($B$21:$M$21)	=C21+4*STDEVA($B$21:$M$21)

Figure 5.4 Formulae for results section of calculation
and processing worksheet

	A	B	C	D	E	F	G
24	WORK AREA						
25							
26	QUARTERS	Q1	Q2	Q3	Q4	Q5	Q6
27	DATA	6500	6950	7200	8500	6900	7200
28	CENTRED MOVING AVERAGE			7337.5	7418.75	7487.5	7425
29	RESIDUALS			0.981260647	1.145745577	0.921535893	0.96969697
30	SEASONAL COMPONENTS	0.94132	0.969263754	1.000248766	1.089168509	0.94131897	0.969263754
31	CENTRING FACTOR	0.99886					
32	INITIAL SEASONAL ESTIMATES	0.94024	0.968155321	0.9991049	1.087922956		
33	CYCLE*RESIDUAL	1.01394	1.032602723	1.017021029	1.082179829	0.997946791	0.993228463
34	W(X)=RESIDUAL-1	0.01394	0.032602723	0.017021029	0.082179829	-0.00205321	-0.00677154
35	W(X)*W(X)	0.00019	0.001062938	0.000289715	0.006753524	4.21567E-06	4.58537E-05
36	W(X)*W(X-1)		0.000454545	0.000554932	0.001398785	-0.00016873	1.39034E-05
37	SUM(W*W)	0.01697					
38	SUM(W(X)*W(X-1))	0.00525					
39	PHI	0.30953					
40							

Figure 5.5 Work area of calculation and processing worksheet

The seasonal components indicate the adjustments that act on the trend due to seasonality. These are expressed as percentages and show, for example, that if the component for season one is 90% then, on average, the value of the series in season one is 90% of the value indicated by the trend. There are precisely as many different seasonal components as there are seasons in the data and so in this example there are four seasons for this quarterly series. The seasonal components repeat each year.

	A	B	C	D	
24	WORK AREA				
25					
26	QUARTERS		Q1	Q2		Q3	
27	DATA	=B4	=C4	=D4	=E4
28	CENTRED MOVING AVERAGE			=1/8*B27+1/4*C27+1/4*D27+1/4*E27+1/8*F27	=1/8*C2
29	RESIDUALS			=D4/D28	=E4/E2
30	SEASONAL COMPONENTS	=$B$32/$B$31	=$C$32/$B$31	=$D$32/$B$31	=$E$32
31	CENTRING FACTOR	=SUM(B32:E32)/4			
32	INITIAL SEASONAL ESTIMATE	=($F$29+$J$29)/2	=($G$29+$K$29)/2	=($H$29+$D$29)/2	=($I$29-
33	CYCLE*RESIDUAL	=B4/(B6*B7)	=C4/(C6*C7)	=D4/(D6*D7)	=E4/(E6
34	W(X)=RESIDUAL-1	=B33-1	=C33-1	=D33-1	=E33-1
35	W(X)*W(X)	=B34*B34	=C34*C34	=D34*D34	=E34*E
36	W(X)*W(X-1)		=C34*B34	=D34*C34	=E34*D
37	SUM(W*W)	=SUM(B35:M35)			
38	SUM(W(X)*W(X-1))	=SUM(C36:M36)			
39	PHI	=B38/B37			
40					

Figure 5.6 Formulae for the work area of the calculation
and processing worksheet

The residuals are also expressed as percentages and represent the deviations from the combined series consisting of trend and seasonal components. Therefore, for example, if the first historical value is 75.9 units and the trend and seasonal components associated with this point in time are 65.0 and 120% respectively, the corresponding residual is calculated as:

$$75.9/(65.0*120\%) = 0.973 = 97.3\%$$

The forecast in row 21 can then be calculated by multiplying the trend by the seasonality by the residual (F=T*S*R) and high and low forecast bounds are calculated in rows 19, 20, 23 and 24.

Graphics

Three charts have been created which illustrate the original data and the seasonally adjusted data, the trend and seasonally adjusted data and the trend line, and the forecast together with the lines for plus and minus two and four standard deviations. Figures 5.7, 5.8 and 5.9 are examples of these charts using the sample data from Figure 5.1.

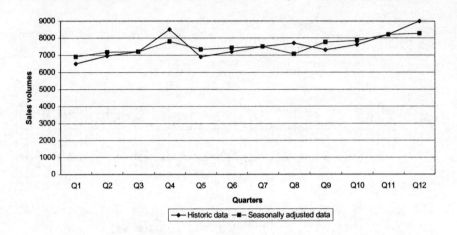

Figure 5.7 Original data and seasonally adjusted data

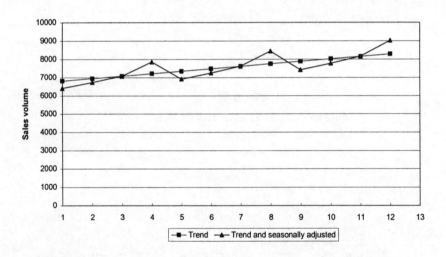

Figure 5.8 Trend and seasonally adjusted data and trend line

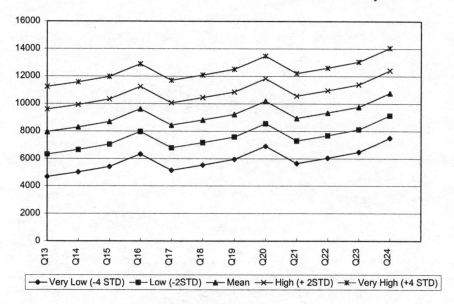

Figure 5.8 Mean forecast and forecast plus and minus two and four
standard deviations

SUMMARY

As already stated the formulae required to develop the multiplicative time series template are not trivial and in order to understand the relationships required a sound knowledge of statistics is necessary.

It is beyond the scope of this book to explain in detail all the formulae used, but rather a general overview of the system has been supplied which will allow the reader to work with the template supplied on the accompanying CD.

6

Expected Values

The affair (investment in business) was partly a lottery, though with the ultimate result largely governed by whether the abilities and character of the managers were above or below the average. Some would fail and some would succeed.

John Maynard Keynes, *The General Theory of Employment, Interest and Money*, Harcourt Brace Jovanovich, San Diego, 1964.

INTRODUCTION

An approach to forecasting which is much more subjective is that of *composite of individual estimates using expected values*. The approach is quite different to all the other techniques described in this book because it does not rely on historic data. The expected value technique requires the opinions of experts as to the likely occurrence of events in the future. These occurrences are estimated in terms of their magnitude as well as in terms of their probability of occurrence.

For example this technique can be used for the evaluation of the probabilities of future sales where there are a large number of clients who are expected to re-purchase from time to time. Because the data will be estimates of expected sales it is important that the sales force maintain close and regular contact with clients and prospects in order that they are in a position to prepare useful estimations. It is also important that the Sales Director responsible for the forecast model is familiar with both the clients and his or her sales team.

A MODEL FOR ANALYSING EXPECTED VALUES

The input required for a model to evaluate the probabilities of future sales is a list of existing clients' and prospects' names, together with estimates of what they are expected to spend on the firms' products over the forecast period. The probability of the sales actually occurring, represented as a percentage value, is entered and the estimated sales value is multiplied by the probability to produce the *expected value*. The expected value for all the clients and prospects is totalled and this value is used as the forecast of the total sales revenue for the forecast period.

Figure 6.1 shows the worksheet on which the data is entered and the expected values are calculated. This data can be found in the file **EXPECT** on the CD accompanying this book. For the purposes of this example only a small sample of data has been used, but in a real business situation this would be much larger. Figure 6.2 shows the formulae required to calculate the totals and the expected values.

	A	B	C	D
1	Forecasting System using Expected Values for January 19XX			
2	Full List of Prospective Sales			
3				
4	Prospect/Client Name	Forecast Sales Value	Probability	Expected Value
5	International Chemicals	250,000	0.20	50,000
6	Forward Motors	30,000	0.10	3,000
7	Penny Bazaar	435,000	0.80	348,000
8	Health Care Concern	960,000	0.90	864,000
9	Futuretown University	250,000	0.50	125,000
10	Century Bank	260,000	0.50	130,000
11	Midlands Transport	350,000	0.40	140,000
12	Flagstone Builders	90,000	0.60	54,000
13	Superflight Airways	110,000	0.40	44,000
14	Global Computers	620,000	0.10	62,000
15	Atlantic Shipping	900,000	0.60	540,000
16	**Total Expected Sales**	**4,255,000**	**0.60**	**2,360,000**

Figure 6.1 Model for analysing expected sales values

	A	B	C	D
1	Forecasting System using			
2	Full List of Prospective Sa			
3				
4	Prospect/Client Name	Forecast Sales Value	Probability	Expected Value
5	International Chemicals	250000	0.2	=B5*C5
6	Forward Motors	30000	0.1	=C6*B6
7	Penny Bazaar	435000	0.8	=C7*B7
8	Health Care Concern	960000	0.9	=C8*B8
9	Futuretown University	250000	0.5	=C9*B9
10	Century Bank	260000	0.5	=C10*B10
11	Midlands Transport	350000	0.4	=C11*B11
12	Flagstone Builders	90000	0.6	=C12*B12
13	Superflight Airways	110000	0.4	=C13*B13
14	Global Computers	620000	0.1	=C14*B14
15	Atlantic Shipping	900000	0.6	=C15*B15
16	Total Expected Sales	=SUM(B5:B15)	=ROUND(D16/B16,1)	=SUM(D5:D15)
17				

Figure 6.2 Cell contents for expected values model

This technique relies on the fact that with a large list of clients and prospects, the probabilities will average themselves out and the end result will be close to the forecast expected value. The formula for the expected value is:

*Expected value = Forecast value * Probability*

Extracting data

Having entered all the data into the spreadsheet it can be used to select subsets of clients based on specified criteria. For example it might be useful to know the clients who are listed with a probability of more than 0.5.

Excel has a feature called Autofilter that can be used for this purpose. Autofilter is switched on by placing the cursor on any of the cells in row 4 and selecting Data Filter Autofilter. This places a small arrow to the right of each column heading in the expected value table. By clicking on the arrow in the Probability column a series of options are displayed which includes Custom. Figure 6.3 shows the custom dialogue box which allows the required criteria to be entered – in this case 'greater than (>) 0.5'.

	A	B	C	D	E	F
1	Forecasting System using Expected Values for January 1998					
2	Full List of Prospective Sales					
3						
4	Prospect/Client Name ▾	Forecast Sales Val ▾	Probabil ▾	Expected Val ▾		
5	International Chemicals	250,000				
6	Forward Motors	30,000				
7	Penny Bazaar	437,013				
8	Health Care Concern	959,666				
9	Futuretown University	250,000				
10	Century Bank	256,902				
11	Midlands Transport	350,000				
12	Flagstone Builders	90,000				
13	Superflight Airways	112,191				
14	Global Computers	619,466				
15	Atlantic Shipping	907,909				
16	Total Expected Sales	4,263,147				

Custom AutoFilter dialogue box overlay:
Show Rows Where: Probability > 0.5 · And / Or · OK · Cancel · Use ? to represent any single character · Use * to represent any series of characters

Figure 6.3 Criteria selection dialogue box

The results of the above query can be seen in Figure 6.4. Notice that the rows containing probability values that do not satisfy the criteria are hidden.

	A	B	C	D
1	Forecasting System using Expected Values for January 1998			
2	Full List of Prospective Sales			
3				
4	Prospect/Client Name ▾	Forecast Sales Val ▾	Probabil ▾	Expected Val ▾
7	Penny Bazaar	437,013	0.80	349,610
8	Health Care Concern	959,666	0.85	815,716
10	Century Bank	256,902	0.55	141,296
12	Flagstone Builders	90,000	0.55	49,500
15	Atlantic Shipping	907,909	0.60	544,745
16	Total Expected Sales	4,263,147	0.55	2,335,691
17				

Figure 6.4 Results of query on probability greater than 0.5

1-2-3 does not have an Autofilter facility, but a similar result is achieved by selecting Tools Database Find and completing the dialogue box shown in Figure 6.5.

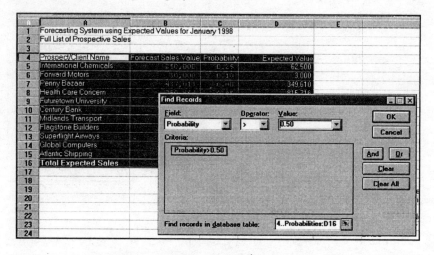

Figure 6.5 Database Find dialogue box in 1-2-3

On selecting OK after completing the dialogue box the items satisfying the criteria are highlighted as shown in Figure 6.6.

If a permanent record is required of items satisfying a particular requirement a report can be produced. In 1-2-3 this is achieved by selecting Tools Database New Query and completing the resulting dialogue box. In Excel the Data Filter Advanced Autofilter command is required which allows the report range and the required criteria to be entered into a dialogue box.

	A	B	C	D
1	Forecasting System using Expected Values for January 1998			
2	Full List of Prospective Sales			
3				
4	Prospect/Client Name	Forecast Sales Value	Probability	Expected Value
5	International Chemicals	250,000	0.25	62,500
6	Forward Motors	30,000	0.10	3,000
7	Penny Bazaar	437,013	0.80	349,610
8	Health Care Concern	959,666	0.85	815,716
9	Futuretown University	250,000	0.49	122,500
10	Century Bank	256,902	0.55	141,296
11	Midlands Transport	350,000	0.40	140,000
12	Flagstone Builders	90,000	0.55	49,500
13	Superflight Airways	112,191	0.40	44,876
14	Global Computers	619,466	0.10	61,947
15	Atlantic Shipping	907,909	0.60	544,745
16	Total Expected Sales	4,263,147	0.55	2,335,691

Figure 6.6 Items satisfying the specified criteria in 1-2-3

SUMMARY

The composite of individual estimates using expected values technique is particularly useful in situations where there are a large number of clients and prospects, and when there is a sales-force who maintain regular and close contact with the client/prospect base.

In these situations, the large number of clients and prospects ensure that the expected value averages out over the whole range, and that the resulting estimation approximately represents the actual sales.

The main problem with this technique is the subjective values involved in setting the probability levels for each client or prospect. If great care is not taken over these figures then the resulting forecast is likely to be of little value.

Selecting and Evaluating Forecasting Techniques

Real problems are hard to spot, especially for managers so involved in day-to-day operations that they have inadequate perspective to see the big picture.

F. Wiersema, *Customer Intimacy*, Knowledge Exchange, Santa Monica, California, 1996.

INTRODUCTION

The preceding chapters of this book have explained in some detail how to prepare forecasts using a range of different methods, tools and techniques. For any forecast to be useful it has to be accurate to an acceptable level and the level of accuracy can be affected considerably by the forecasting approach that is taken. This chapter provides a table of different forecasting techniques and indicates when they are suitable. Some guidelines are given as to how to measure the level of accuracy after a forecast has been calculated.

SELECTING THE RIGHT TECHNIQUE

Table 7.1 provides a list of the forecasting techniques described in this book and evaluates them under the following sections:

- appropriate use;
- time horizon;
- maths sophistication;
- data required.

The techniques described are not an exhaustive list of forecasting techniques, but cover those most suited to the spreadsheet environment which have already bern explained in this book.

Technique	Use	Maths	Data
Moving averages	Repeated forecasts without seasonality	A minimal level of competency	Historic data essential
Adaptive filtering	Repeated forecasts without seasonality and where the nature of any trend may change over time	Some statistical knowledge is required	Historic data essential, but level and detail can vary
Exponential smoothing	Repeated forecast with or without seasonality	Some statistical knowledge to set up a system but virtually none to operate a well-designed system	Only recent data and current forecast is required once the smoothing factor is established
Simple linear regression	Comparing one independent variable with one dependent variable where there is a linear relationship between the variables	Some statistical knowledge to set up a system but virtually none to operate a well-designed system	A sample of relevant observations for the independent and dependent variables
Multiple linear regression	When more than one independent variables is to be compared with a dependent variable	Some statistical knowledge is required	A sample of relevant observations for the independent and dependent variables

Technique	Use	Maths	Data
Trend analysis	Forecasting over time in a non-linear way using simple regression	Some statistical competence is required	Historic data with as much detail as possible
Decomposition analysis	Identify seasonal components as part of another forecasting method	Requires statistical knowledge to set up a system but virtually none to operate a well-designed system	Historic data for the one variable under consideration is required
Composite of individual estimates	Forecasting using a large number of individual estimates	No statistics and only basic arithmetic required	Past data not required

Table 7.1 Different forecasting techniques

ACCURACY AND RELIABILITY

Every forecast should include an estimate of its accuracy and an assessment of its reliability. This not only allows for a reasonable and acceptable margin of error, but also helps to build confidence in the methods being used, and the results achieved.

Many forecasts are repetitive, being prepared either weekly or monthly. This provides an invaluable source of forecast assessment data, since the forecasts' predictions can be measured against the reality, and can then be adjusted with the benefit of hindsight. Explicit analysis will highlight weak spots in the forecast, and improve the accuracy of future forecasts.

The three primary approaches to evaluating the accuracy of a forecast are to use graphics, quantitative (statistical) analysis and subjective methods.

GRAPHICS

Graphical methods are particularly useful when it is necessary to identify potential problems as early as possible. Control charts are the most frequently used graphical method, and these are useful for identifying when a forecast method requires adjustment. Prediction realisation diagrams are another graphical method to consider.

STATISTICAL METHODS

Quantitative or statistical methods are useful for comparing different forecasting methods, and in estimating confidence limits. A confidence limit is a specification that combines a statement about a point estimate with a measure of the precision of that estimate.

Average error

The *average error*, or the *average absolute error* or the *mean absolute error*, is the simplest of all to compute. The algebraic formula is:

$$Average\,error = (\left|(F_1 - A_1)\right| + \left|(F_2 + A_2)\right| + ... + \left|(F_t - A_t)\right|) / T$$

where F_t = forecast for period t, A_t = actual value for period t, T = number of forecasts to be used, and the modulus ($|\,|$) means that the absolute value is to be used. In other words if the value is negative, its sign should be changed to positive.

Once computed, the average error for a particular forecasting method can be compared with the average errors for another method. Alternatively the average error for different time periods can be calculated and compared. Although the average error does not have any intrinsic statistical property that makes it useful for the estimation of confidence limits, it is a useful indication as to the accuracy of a forecast.

Standard error

The most widely used measure of forecasting accuracy is the standard error and this technique was used in Chapter 6 in conjunction with the regression analysis.

The standard error is particularly useful because it can be used to compute confidence limits and, because the terms are squared, it places more emphasis on large errors. There are however some pre-requisites for the use of standard errors:

1. the error terms are normally distributed. A normal distribution is a model of a continuous variable whose value depends upon the effect of a number of factors, each factor exerting a small positive or negative influence;
2. the average forecasting error is zero, i.e. there is no tendency to regularly over or under-estimate;
3. the errors are not serially correlated, i.e. the error terms do not show a pattern, in terms of direction or size, over time.

If all these conditions are met, then 68% of the outcomes will be within plus or minus one standard error, 95% will be within plus or minus twice the standard error, and 99.7% will be within plus or minus three times the standard error.

The control chart will show whether there is any pattern in the error terms, and calculation of the error terms will show whether they meet the necessary conditions as a basis for computation of the confidence limits.

Thiels U

Thiels U compares the accuracy of a forecasting model to a naïve model that uses the last period's outcome to predict the present period's outcome. This is using what is already known to predict the future and is thus a measure of relative accuracy. U is defined by:

$$U = \frac{\text{(Standard error of forecasting model)}}{\text{(Standard error of naïve model)}}$$

Values of U greater than one indicate that the method of forecasting selected was worse than the naïve model; values less than one indicate that it was better.

U can also be used to compare the accuracy of various forecasting methods, or even to compare the accuracy of one method over different time-spans. This is useful when selecting the optimum time-span or period for a forecast.

SUBJECTIVE METHODS

Subjective forecasting methods are based on common sense. They involve using a measure of judgement and self-expertise in the evaluation of a forecast.

When applying subjective methods it is important to avoid *spurious correlations* which refers to correlations where the associations are real enough, but misinterpretation of the results, or unwise jumping to conclusions, has led to erroneous conclusions being drawn from the forecast.

The original assumptions under which the predictions were made, and upon which the model was built, should be kept in mind. If a factor is considered to be particularly critical, then different forecasts can be prepared using alternative assumptions.

No matter how well the forecast has performed in the past, the model itself and its underlying assumptions should be periodically re-examined in order to ensure that the same conditions prevail.

SUMMARY

As success at forecasting is an important contributor to the firm's performance, time and effort should be applied to ensure that a suitable forecasting technique is being used. This will certainly result in costs of various types being minimised.

All three methods discussed in this chapter are important and can be applied individually or collectively depending on the precise situation.

Part Two

$$\boxed{8}$$

Business Planning

Planning, of course is not a separate, recognizable act.... Every managerial act, mental or physical is inexorably intertwined with planning. It is as much a part of every managerial act as breathing is to the living human.'

C. George, *The History of Management*, Prentice-Hall, 1972.

INTRODUCTION

If business forecasting involves the prediction of what could happen in the future, business planning involves the calculation of what is required to fulfil the forecast, i.e. make the future happen as it is forecast. Thus a business plan uses a forecast as an initial point of departure and then adds considerable detail to reflect how the particular process or project is intended to proceed. Plans are generally set in the future and involve making a series of assumptions about how the variables in the plan will behave in future periods.

Business plans are used to help with decision making. There are many types of business plan, which range from simple verbal or written descriptions of what is to be achieved, through diagrammatic representations such as Gantt charts to highly analytical numeric reports.

There are many definitions of planning, but perhaps one worth quoting is from Ackoff[1] who said:

> Planning is required when the future state that we desire involves a set of interdependent decisions; that is, a system of decisions ... The principal complexity in planning derives from the interrelatedness of the decisions rather than from the decisions themselves ...

In the context of this book, a business plan is a statement of quantifiable objectives, together with the resources required to achieve them. The objective may be profit, market share, return on investment or cash flow, to mention only a few, and the resources could be manpower, materials, capital, cash, etc.

There are many different ways of classifying business plans, including short-term, long-term, profit plans, marketing plans, production plans, personnel development plans, capital investment plans, merger and take-over plans, etc. The detail supplied in the plan reflects the ultimate use for which it is intended. For high level strategic decisions, plans often contain little detail, while for operational planning a large amount of detail is usually required. The contents will reflect the nature of the project or process being planned, but it is not unusual for operational plans to involve dozens of line items. These types of plan often forms the basis of a financial budget, which in some cases is no more than a plan divided into specific responsibility points and specific time periods.

An important aspect of business planning is *what-if analysis*. This is the process of changing one or more of the assumptions on which a business plan has been based in order to see what effect such a change in circumstances would have on the results. This subject is covered in detail in Chapter 12.

---

[1] R. L. Ackoff, *A Concept of Corporate Planning*, Wiley, New York, 1970.

APPROACHES TO BUSINESS PLANNING

There are three generically different approaches to developing business plans, which are described as *deterministic*[2], *stochastic*[3] or *probabilistic*, and *optimising*.

Deterministic planning

Deterministic planning is the most frequently encountered. It is the basis on which virtually all corporate budgeting is performed. A deterministic plan takes single values that are the best estimate for the variables in the plan and uses this value with a set of logic rules to produce the plan or budget. The single start value for a line item in a plan is referred to as a *point estimate*. Although it is recognised by planners and budgeting officers that accurate point estimates are almost impossible to obtain, it is believed that they are sufficiently accurate to be useful. This value will in many cases be the result of a forecasting plan such as those described in Part One of this book.

The method of planning is called 'deterministic' because once the point estimates are derived, the outcome of the plan may be uniquely determined by the logic, i.e. there will be only one answer. For example, consider the following:

Sales volume	*100*	
Unit price	*50*	
Revenue	*5000*	*(Sales volume * Unit price)*

The only way a different result can be obtained in the above example is by changing one of the single point estimates. Of course, one of the great advantages of the spreadsheet is that making changes to opening data, growth rates, cost factors etc.,

---

[2] According to the *American Heritage Dictionary of the English Language*, Third Edition, deterministic refers to the fact that there is an inevitable consequence of antecedents.

[3] According to the *American Heritage Dictionary of the English Language*, Third Edition, stochastic refers to involving a random variable or variables and the chance or probability of their occurrence.

causes all directly and indirectly affected cells to recalculate and thus different scenarios can be sort. However the basic principle is that the outcome is uniquely determined by the logic.

Figure 8.1 is a simple profit and loss plan that has been developed in a typical deterministic fashion. Figure 8.2 shows the formulae used for the plan.

	A	B	C	D	E	F
1	Profit and Loss Account for 4 Quarterly periods					
2						
3		1st qtr	2nd qtr	3rd qtr	4th qtr	Total
4						
5	Sales Volume	6000	6180	6365	6556	25101
6	Unit Price	10.00	10.20	10.40	10.61	
7	Sales Turnover	60000	63036	66221	69573	258830
8						
9	Material Costs	24000	24720	25460	26224	100404
10	Labour	10000	10150	10302	10457	40909
11	Energy Expenses	8000	8160	8323	8489	32972
12	Total Direct Costs	42000	43030	44085	45170	174285
13						
14	Gross Profit	18000	20006	22136	24403	84545
15						
16	Administration	1500	1576	1656	1739	6471
17	Depreciation	1500	1500	1500	1500	6000
18	Finance Charges	1200	1200	1200	1200	4800
19	Maintenance	600	630	662	696	2588
20	Salary Expenses	13000	13780	14607	15483	56870
21	Total Other Costs	17800	18686	19625	20618	76729
22						
23	Net Profit B.T.	200	1320	2512	3785	7816

Figure 8.1 A typical deterministic plan

	A	B	C	D	E	F
1						
2						
3		*1st qtr*	*2nd qtr*	*3rd qtr*	*4th qtr*	*Total*
4	Sales Volume	6000	=B4*1.03	=C4*1.03	=D4*1.03	=SUM(B4:E4)
5	Unit Price	10	=B5*1.02	=C5*1.02	=D5*1.02	
6	**Sales Turnover**	=B4*B5	=C4*C5	=D4*D5	=E4*E5	=SUM(B6:E6)
7						
8	Material Costs	=B4*4	=C4*4	=D4*4	=E4*4	=SUM(B8:E8)
9	Labour	10000	=B9*1.015	=C9*1.015	=D9*1.015	=SUM(B9:E9)
10	Energy Expenses	8000	=B10*1.02	=C10*1.02	=D10*1.02	=SUM(B10:E10)
11	**Total Direct Costs**	=SUM(B8:B10)	=SUM(C8:C10)	=SUM(D8:D10)	=SUM(E8:E10)	=SUM(B11:E11)
12						
13	**Gross Profit**	=B6-B11	=C6-C11	=D6-D11	=E6-E11	=SUM(B13:E13)
14						
15	Administration	=B6*0.025	=C6*0.025	=D6*0.025	=E6*0.025	=SUM(B15:E15)
16	Depreciation	1500	=B16	=C16	=D16	=SUM(B16:E16)
17	Finance Charges	1200	1200	1200	1200	=SUM(B17:E17)
18	Maintenance	=B6*0.01	=C6*0.01	=D6*0.01	=E6*0.01	=SUM(B18:E18)
19	Salary Expenses	13000	=B19*1.06	=C19*1.06	=D19*1.06	=SUM(B19:E19)
20	**Total Other Costs**	=SUM(B15:B19)	=SUM(C15:C19)	=SUM(D15:D19)	=SUM(E15:E19)	=SUM(B20:E20)
21						
22	**Net Profit B.T.**	=B13-B20	=C13-C20	=D13-D20	=E13-E20	=SUM(B22:E22)

Figure 8.2 Formulae for the typical deterministic plan

Stochastic planning

A stochastic or probabilistic plan recognises that because point estimates are difficult to accurately establish, it is quite often better to establish ranges into which it is thought values will fall. Thus, for example, in a stochastic plan, rather than using a point estimate of £50,000 as an opening sales value, a range consisting of values of between, say £45,000 and £52,500 could be entered. Similar ranges could be entered for other line items in the plan.

Probabilities are then associated with the data input ranges and the computer recalculates the plan thousands of times using values within the specified range to produce a large number of results, or scenarios, which correspond to different possible outcomes. This method is referred to as the *Monte Carlo* method. It is frequently used to evaluate large capital investment alternatives of complex marketing situations. Because this type of planning is concerned with attributing the probability of a particular outcome it is often referred to as *risk analysis*.

There are a number of different probability distribution techniques that can be applied to stochastic planning, including uniform, triangular and beta. The examples shown in this book will assume a uniform distribution.

Because stochastic planning requires a reiterative process to collect thousands of alternative results, it requires considerable computing power that did not used to be available on desk-top computers and thus was not considered a spreadsheet application. However with the powerful PCs that are commonplace today, stochastic planning has become a relatively simple application to develop.

The detail of how to set up and work with a stochastic plan for risk analysis is given in Chapter 12, but the underlying logic required to apply stochastic analysis to the deterministic plan shown in Figure 8.1 using a uniform or normal distribution is as follows:

Sales volume	*Random * (high–low)+low*
Unit price	*Random * (high–low)+low*
Revenue	*Sales volume * Unit price*

The input data for the above model might be:

	High	Low
Sales volume	*52,000*	*45,000*
Unit price	*43*	*35*

The use of a random selection from the range provides a normal, uniform or rectangular distribution, but other distributions such as binomial, poisson or triangular could be specified.

Figure 8.3 shows a typical data input form for a stochastic plan and Figure 8.4 shows some of the formulae required. Although the input form allows ranges to be specified for all the line items in the profit and loss plan, for this example only the sales volume and the Unit Price have been used. For the purposes of Figure 8.4 values for the remaining variables have been included in the formulae. The results of risk analysis are usually best viewed graphically and an example is shown in Figure 8.5.

	A	B	C	D	E	F
1	Data Input for Risk Analysis					
2		Opening Value			Growth Rate	
3		Minimum	Maximum		Minimum	Maximum
4	**Income**					
5	Sales Volume	5800	6250		2.00%	4.00%
6	Unit Price	9.75	10.50		1.00%	4.00%
7						
8	**Direct Costs**					
9	Material Costs					
10	Labour					
11	Energy Expenses					
12						
13	**Indirect Costs**					
14	Administration					
15	Depreciation					
16	Finance Charges					
17	Maintenance					
18	Salary Expenses					
19						

Figure 8.3 Input form for risk analysis

	A	B	C
2			
3		*1st qtr*	*2nd qtr*
4			
5	Sales Volume	=Inputs!$B5+RAND()*(Inputs!$C5-Inputs!$B5)	=B5*(1+Inputs!$E5+RAND()*(Inputs!$F5-Inputs!$E5))
6	Unit Price	=Inputs!$B6+RAND()*(Inputs!$C6-Inputs!$B6)	=B6*(1+Inputs!$E6+RAND()*(Inputs!$F6-Inputs!$E6))
7	**Sales Turnover**	=B5*B6	=C5*C6
8			
9	Material Costs	=B5*4	=C5*4
10	Labour	10000	=B10*1.015
11	Energy Expenses	8000	=B11*1.02
12	Total Direct Costs	=SUM(B9:B11)	=SUM(C9:C11)
13			
14	*Gross Profit*	=B7-B12	=C7-C12
15			
16	Administration	=B7*0.025	=C7*0.025
17	Depreciation	1500	=B17
18	Finance Charges	1200	1200
19	Maintenance	=B7*0.01	=C7*0.01
20	Salary Expenses	13000	=B20*1.06
21	*Total Other Costs*	=SUM(B16:B20)	=SUM(C16:C20)
22			
23	**Net Profit B.T.**	=B14-B21	=C14-C21
24			

Plan / Inputs / Risk Results / Graphical Results /

Figure 8.4 Formulae required for risk analysis

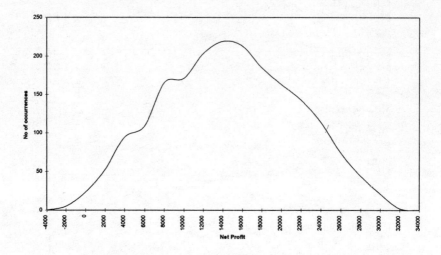

Figure 8.5 Graph showing results of risk analysis

From the graph in Figure 8.5 it can be seen that, given all the assumptions in the underlying model, the most likely outcome is a net profit of about £14,000. However, given the ranges of input data it is possible for the net profit to be as bad as a £4000 loss or it could possibly be a profit as high as £34,000.

More detail on how to interpret the results of risk analysis is given in Chapter 12.

Optimising models

Optimising models attempt to find a unique course of action that will produce the best result, given a set of restraints. One of the most frequently encountered optimising models in business is the economic order quantity model, whereby the most cost-effective order quantities are calculated. An optimising model always attempts to match an objective within a given set of restraints and the spreadsheet *Solver* feature makes this type of analysis possible within the spreadsheet environment.

Backward iteration or goal seeking is another popular form of optimising model whereby the computer calculates the course of action that must be undertaken in order to achieve a particular objective. In this case it is usual to change only one variable as a time and constraints are not always necessary. The spreadsheet features *Goal Seek* or *Backsolver* facilitate this type of analysis.

Table 8.1 shows the three types of business plans together with their primary use and development features.

Type of Plan	Primary Use	Features
Deterministic	Income and expenditure, budgeting	Extrapolation of formulae and constraints
Risk or stochastic	Complex capital investment appraisal	Exploration of multiple scenarios
Optimising	Finding the unique course of action to produce the optimal result	Solving a series of equations representing operational constraints

Table 8.1 Summary of business planning approaches

SUMMARY

Before embarking on the development of any spreadsheet application it is important to take time to consider what type of plan is required and the best approach for the design and structure of the plan. The following chapters in Part Two of this book describe the techniques required for the development of deterministic, stochastic and optimising models, as well as how to get the most out of the plans through what-if analysis.

9

Spreadsheet Skills for all Types of Planning

The most popularly claimed pitfall of planning concerns commitment. The assumption is that with the support and participation of the top management, all will be well. But the questions must be asked: well with what and well for whom? For planners? To be sure. But for the organisation?

Henry Mintzberg, *The Rise and Fall of Strategic Planning*, The Free Press, 1994.

INTRODUCTION

Whether a spreadsheet is being developed as a forecasting plan, a profit and loss account or a marketing plan it is essential that due care and attention be given to the design and structure of the plan. Establishing some rules as to how all the spreadsheets in a department or organisation are developed enables different people to look at different plans and feel familiar with the layout, style, reports, charts, etc. This is in much the same way as users feel familiar with different software applications that have a similar interface. Microsoft Office and Lotus SmartSuite are two such examples.

The objectives of good design in spreadsheet terms are exactly the same as those required for any other software development:

1. to ensure that the spreadsheet is as error free as possible;

2. to ensure that the spreadsheet may easily be used without much training or control;
3. to minimise the work required to enhance or change the spreadsheet.

If care is taken to ensure sound structure and good design a spreadsheet will be straightforward to develop, easy to read, simple to use, not difficult to change and will produce the required results.

The plan developed over a number of developmental stages in this chapter illustrates a variety of aspects of the principles of spreadsheet design and development. The series begins with a plan that has had little or no thought put into its design and layout and as the chapter proceeds ways of improving and enhancing the plan are identified and explained. These plans can be found on the CD accompanying the book under the names STYLE01 through STYLE10.

SPREADSHEET 1

The spreadsheet in Figure 9.1 is a simple profit projection that may be of use to the author, but is unlikely to be helpful to anyone else. This is clearly a quick one-off plan which has been prepared with very little care and which may well not even be saved on the disk.

	A	B	C	D	E
1	sales	150	173	198	228
2	price	12.55	12.55	12.55	12.55
3	revenue	1883	2165	2490	2863
4	costs	1185	1362	1567	1802
5	profit	698	803	923	1061
6					

Figure 9.1 Simple profit projection

Problems with this spreadsheet

The immediately obvious problems with this spreadsheet are that it has no title, it is not clear what the columns represent, i.e. are they different periods or perhaps different products, and the author is unknown.

With regards the data itself, the figures are hard to read as there are varying numbers of decimal places. Whilst perhaps there has been a growth in sales and price, the percentage has not been indicated. The costs line could be misleading as no indication of where the costs have been derived is supplied.

Positive aspects of this spreadsheet

If the author of the spreadsheet required a quick profit estimation based on known data and growth rates for sales units, price and costs then the spreadsheet has supplied that information quickly and in a more concise form than would have been achievable using a calculator and recording the results on paper.

SPREADSHEET 2

In Figure 9.2 the three major shortfalls of the first spreadsheet have been remedied. However there is still plenty of room for improvement.

	A	B	C	D	E
1	Profit Projection for Widget Division for 1998				
2	Written by P.A. Jones 31 July 1997				
3					
4		Qtr 1	Qtr 2	Qtr 3	Qtr 4
5	sales	150	175	195	220
6	price	12.55	12.55	12.55	12.55
7	revenue	1882.5	2196.25	2447.25	2761
8	costs	1184.55	1381.975	1539.915	1737.34
9	profit	697.95	814.275	907.335	1023.66
10					

Figure 9.2 Incorporating some annotation

Problems with this spreadsheet

The construction of the data and results is still unclear and the lack of formatting makes the figures hard to read. The costs remain grouped together.

Positive aspects of this spreadsheet

In addition to the name of the author having been added to the plan, the date when the plan was written is a useful feature. The date becomes particularly important when the question of spreadsheet versions arise. Note that the date has been entered here as text. If a date function had been used it would be continually updated each time the file is retrieved, whereas here it is the date of the last update that is required. It is also very useful if the author supplies information as to how he or she may be located, perhaps by supplying a telephone number. The ruling lines above and below specific sections of the spreadsheet are also quite helpful. This can be quickly achieved using the automatic formatting features, or tailored spreadsheet styles can be designed which incorporate corporate style.

SPREADSHEET 3

Totals and/or summary data is very important in any business report. Thus in Figure 9.3 the data for the four quarters is totalled and reported as an annual figure. The values in the plan have also been formatted with the majority of figures being formatted to zero decimal places and the price line to two decimal places.

One of the automatic formatting options has been selected to shade and outline the plan.

	A	B	C	D	E	F
1	Profit Projection for Widget Division for 1998					
2	Written by P.A. Jones 31 July 1997					
3						
4		Qtr 1	Qtr 2	Qtr 3	Qtr 4	Total
5	sales	150	173	198	228	749
6	price	12.55	12.55	12.55	12.55	
7	revenue	1883	2165	2490	2863	9400
8	costs	1185	1362	1567	1802	5915
9	profit	698	803	923	1061	3485
10						
11						
12	Report Printed		13-Jan-98	14:44:00		

Figure 9.3 Incorporating totals into the plan

Problems with this spreadsheet

Constants or raw data exist in this spreadsheet both for opening values for sales and price as well as for growth rates and unit costs. This leads to a number of difficulties, especially with respect to future what-if analysis.

Furthermore, having constants embedded in the spreadsheet, especially as growth factors, makes understanding the assumptions in the spreadsheet more difficult because the values cannot be seen without positioning the cursor on the cells where the growth factors are referenced.

Positive aspects of this spreadsheet

Having a current date and time indicator displayed on the spreadsheet ensures that a hard copy report will reflect the date, and perhaps more importantly the time it was printed. This is achieved through the DATE function that can be formatted with a range of different display options. Because it is likely that a spreadsheet will be recalculated, even if it is set to manual calculation, before printing, the date and time will always be up-to-date.

The cells in this version of the spreadsheet have now been formatted which makes the data easier to read. When formatting a spreadsheet it is important to consider the entire plan and not just the cells that are currently being worked on. The entire spreadsheet should be formatted to the degree of accuracy the majority of the plan is to be and those cells that need to be different, such as percentages, can be reformatted when necessary.

It is important to understand that formatting cells only changes the display and does not affect the results of calculations that are still performed to the full degree of accuracy, which is usually 16 significant decimal places. It is for this reason that a cell containing the sum of a range of cells might display a different answer to what the user would calculate by visually adding up the values as they are displayed on the screen.

To ensure that the results of a calculation are rounded to, for example, zero decimal places, the ROUND function must be applied to the formulae generating the results. Figure 9.4 shows two tables representing the same extract from a profit and loss account. In both cases all the cells have been formatted to zero decimal places, but in Table B the ROUND function has been incorporated in the formulae for cells F15 through F20.

The formula entered into cell F15, which can then be copied for the other line items is:

ROUND(SUM(B15:E15),0)

	A	B	C	D	E	F
14	Costs					
15	Administration	1500	1576	1656	1739	6471
16	Depreciation	1500	1553	1607	1663	6322
17	Finance Charges	1200	1288	1382	1482	5352
18	Maintenance	600	630	662	696	2588
19	Salary Expenses	13000	13858	14773	15748	57378
20	*Total Other Costs*	17800	18904	20079	21328	78112
21						
22	Net Profit B.T.	200	1102	2060	3076	6438
23						

Table A

	A	B	C	D	E	F
14	Costs					
15	Administration	1500	1576	1656	1739	6471
16	Depreciation	1500	1553	1607	1663	6322
17	Finance Charges	1200	1288	1382	1482	5352
18	Maintenance	600	630	662	696	2588
19	Salary Expenses	13000	13858	14773	15748	57378
20	*Total Other Costs*	17800	18904	20079	21328	78111
21						
22	Net Profit B.T.	200	1102	2060	3076	6438
23						

Table B

Figure 9.4 Difference between rounding and formatting cells

The effect of the ROUND function can be seen in cell F20. By visually adding up the numbers in the range F15 through F19 the result is 78111 whereas the formatting of these cells without the use of the ROUND function in Table A returns a value of 78112 in cell F20.

SPREADSHEET 4

The provision of a hard copy report showing the logic used to create a plan is most helpful. Care must be given to the width of the cells, otherwise the formulae will be truncated. If formulae are very wide they may be listed using a print option.

In Excel the commands to display the formulae is Tools Options View and then check the Formulas box. There is no option in Excel to display formulae for a selected range. In 1-2-3 a range must be selected and then the command is Style Number Format Text. Figure 9.5 is an example of a spreadsheet displaying the actual cell contents, as opposed to the results of the formulae.

In addition to providing valuable documentation for a spreadsheet system, looking at the contents of the cells as opposed to the results can also be a helpful auditing tool. For example Figure 9.5 highlights the fact that there are still values embedded in formulae which is not good practice and is addressed in the next version of the plan.

	A	B	C	D	E	F
1	Profit Projection					
2	Written by P.A					
3						
4		Qtr 1	Qtr 2	Qtr 3	Qtr 4	Total
5	sales	150	=B5*1.15	=C5*1.15	=D5*1.15	=SUM(B5:E5)
6	price	12.55	12.55	12.55	12.55	
7	revenue	=B5*B6	=C5*C6	=D5*D6	=E5*E6	=SUM(B7:E7)
8	costs	=B5*7.897	=C5*7.897	=D5*7.897	=E5*7.897	=SUM(B8:E8)
9	profit	=B7-B8	=C7-C8	=D7-D8	=E7-E8	=SUM(B9:E9)
10						
11						
12						
13	Report Printed		=NOW()			

Figure 9.5 Report showing formulae

SPREADSHEET 5

One of the reasons that spreadsheets have been enormously successful is the fact that they facilitate quick, easy and inexpensive what-if analysis. What-if analysis may be defined as the process of investigating the effect of changes to assumptions on the objective function of a business plan.

Performing what-if analysis on the opening sales assumption or the opening price assumption is quite straightforward, involving placing the cursor on the figure and entering the new value. On pressing ENTER the spreadsheet is re-evaluated and all cells which refer to the changed values, either directly or indirectly are updated.

The success of performing even the simplest what-if analysis is dependent on the spreadsheet having been developed with the correct series of relationships. For example, changing the opening sales value in Figure 9.6 would automatically cause the other quarter sales values to recalculate, as well as the revenue, costs and profit lines, because they relate, through the cell references in the formulae, either directly or indirectly to the sales value in cell B5.

However, the spreadsheet in Figure 9.6 as it has so far been developed presents problems when what-if analysis is to be performed on the unit price row.

	A	B	C	D	E	F
1	Profit Projection for Widget Division for 1998					
2	Written by P.A. Jones 31 July 1997					
3						
4		Qtr 1	Qtr 2	Qtr 3	Qtr 4	Total
5	sales	350	403	463	532	1748
6	price	12.55	12.55	12.55	12.55	
7	revenue	4393	5051	5809	6680	21933
8	costs	2764	3179	3655	4204	13801
9	profit	1629	1873	2154	2477	8132
10						
11	Report Printed	13-Jan-98	14:52:14			
12						

Figure 9.6 Value references preventing what-if analysis

Problems with this spreadsheet

Because no growth in the price is required the opening value of 12.55 has been copied for the four quarters (this can be seen in Figure 9.5). Whilst this is fine all the time a price of 12.55 is required, it presents a problem when the price requires changing. With this spreadsheet it would be necessary to overwrite the price in the first quarter and then copy the new value for the remaining three quarters.

SPREADSHEET 6

To prevent the problem in Spreadsheet 5 from arising, a relationship should be entered into cell C6 that refers to the value in B6. With such a relationship in place any change to the opening price will immediately be reflected for the remaining quarters. Figure 9.7 shows how the Unit Price in row six of the above spreadsheet should be developed.

	A	B	C	D	E	F
1	Profit Projection					
2	Written by P.A					
3						
4		Qtr 1	Qtr 2	Qtr 3	Qtr 4	Total
5	sales	150	=B5*1.15	=C5*1.15	=D5*1.15	=SUM(B5:E5)
6	price	12.55	=B6	=C6	=D6	

Figure 9.7 Using cell references for non-changing values

SPREADSHEET 7

The spreadsheet as shown in Figure 9.7 still does not lend itself to effective what-if analysis on the growth rates for sales or price. To change these variables the cell containing the first reference to the growth rate would have to be edited to change the value. Then the new relationships in that cell would have to be copied to the end of the range.

This process may be made far more elegant by removing the growth factors from the main body of the spreadsheet and placing them in a more convenient location and then referencing them by the appropriate cells in the main plan. To achieve this the formulae for the second quarter's sales and price must be changed to reference the growth factor. The reference to the cell containing the growth factor must be an *absolute* reference, which means when the formula is copied to the remaining quarters the reference will remain fixed to the growth rate cell. This is achieved by preceding the row and column references with a dollar sign ($) which of course has nothing to do with money value. For example $B$12. Figure 9.8 shows the spreadsheet after making these changes.

	A	B	C	D	E	F
1	Profit Projection for Widget Division for 1996					
2	Written by P.A. Jones 31 July 1995					
3						
4		Qtr 1	Qtr 2	Qtr 3	Qtr 4	Total
5	sales	150	173	198	228	749
6	price	12.55	13.18	13.84	14.53	
7	revenue	1883	2273	2745	3314	10215
8	costs	1125	1294	1488	1711	5618
9	profit	758	979	1257	1603	4597
10						
11						
12	Growth in Sales Volume as %			15%		
13	Growth in Price as %			5%		
14	Cost per unit of production			7.50		
15						
16	Report Printed	13-Jan-98	14:57:58			

Figure 9.8 Removing growth and cost factors from
the main body of the plan

Problems with this spreadsheet

The plan still requires further development for cost factors, etc.

Positive aspects of this spreadsheet

Another benefit gained by removing the growth factors from the main spreadsheet is that they can be seen without having to place the cursor on a particular cell in order to see what the growth rate is. This is the first step in developing a data input form which will ultimately separate all the input data from the actual logic of the spreadsheet. This separation of the data allows the logic cells to be protected from accidental damage.

Figure 9.9 shows the formulae that reference the growth and cost factors once they have been separated from the main body of the spreadsheet.

	A	B	C	D	E	F
1	Profit Projectio					
2	Written by P.A					
3						
4			Qtr 1	Qtr 2	Qtr 3	Qtr 4	Total
5	sales	150	=B5*(1+$D$12)	=C5*(1+$D$12)	=D5*(1+$D$12)	=SUM(B5:E5)
6	price	12.55	=B6*(1+$D$13)	=C6*(1+$D$13)	=D6*(1+$D$13)	
7	revenue	=B5*B6	=C5*C6	=D5*D6	=E5*E6	=SUM(B7:E7)
8	costs	=B5*$D$14	=C5*$D$14	=D5*$D$14	=E5*$D$14	=SUM(B8:E8)
9	profit	=B7-B8	=C7-C8	=D7-D8	=E7-E8	=SUM(B9:E9)
10						
11						
12	Growth in Sale			0.15		
13	Growth in Price			0.05		
14	Cost per unit o			7.5		
15						
16	Report Printed	=NOW()	=NOW()			

Figure 9.9 Amended logic reflecting externally referenced growth and cost factors

SPREADSHEET 8

The amount of detail supplied in the plan so far is clearly insufficient for any real decision making process.

More detail of the firm's cost structure would constitute an obvious improvement and this has been incorporated as a separate section on the plan in Figure 9.10. Wherever possible try and divide plans into sections that fit comfortably on the screen, and indicate that there is more information to follow.

SPREADSHEET 9

Some spreadsheet users would find the spreadsheet in Figure 9.10 disjointed with revenue in one section and the costs in another. Although good spreadsheet design is essential, personal preference will always have a role to play in the finished result, and of course the way in which a system is used and for what purpose will play an important role as to what variables are grouped together. For example, it is not difficult to restructure this spreadsheet as shown in Figure 9.11.

Profit Projection for Widget Division for 1998					
Written by P.A. Jones 31 July 1997					
	Qtr 1	Qtr 2	Qtr 3	Qtr 4	Total
Sales Volume	2575	2961	3405	3916	12858
Price	17.98	18.88	19.82	20.81	
Revenue	46299	55905	67506	81513	251223
Costs	39035	41530	44439	47837	172840
Profit	7264	14376	23067	33677	78383
Factors					
Growth in Sales Volume as %		15%			
Growth in Price as %		5%			
Report Printed	13-Jan-98	15:06:43	[PgDn] for Cost Analysis		
Cost Analysis					
	Qtr 1	Qtr 2	Qtr 3	Qtr 4	Total
Raw Materials	14987	17234	19820	22793	74833
Labour	10000	10000	10000	10000	40000
Energy	798	1045	1369	1794	5007
Depreciation	750	750	750	750	3000
Total Direct Costs	26535	29030	31939	35337	122840
Overheads	12500	12500	12500	12500	50000
Total costs	39035	41530	44439	47837	172840
Factors					
Unit Raw Material		5.82			
Energy increase		31%			

Figure 9.10 Expanded cost structure

	Qtr 1	Qtr 2	Qtr 3	Qtr 4	Total
Profit Projection for Widget Division for 1998					
Written by P.A. Jones 31 July 1997					
	Qtr 1	Qtr 2	Qtr 3	Qtr 4	Total
Sales Volume	2575	2961	3405	3916	12858
Price	17.98	18.88	19.82	20.81	
Revenue	46299	55905	67506	81513	251223
Raw Materials	14987	17234	19820	22793	74833
Labour	10000	10000	10000	10000	40000
Energy	798	1045	1369	1794	5007
Depreciation	750	750	750	750	3000
Total Direct Costs	26535	29030	31939	35337	122840
Overheads	12500	12500	12500	12500	50000
Total costs	39035	41530	44439	47837	172840
Profit	7264	14376	23067	33677	78383
Factors					
Growth in Sales Volume as %			15%		
Growth in Price as %			5%		
Unit Raw Material			5.82		
Energy increase			31%		
Report printed	27-Jun-97	15:17:21			

Figure 9.11 Alternative approach for expanding costs

Problems with this spreadsheet

As far as this plan goes it is quite well designed in that it has a title and a declared author; the cells have been appropriately formatted and the growth and cost factors have been extracted from the main body of the plan.

If this were a large report it would probably be a retrograde step to consolidate the cost details into the overall report. Large systems should be treated in the opposite manner, i.e. modularised where possible. Modules can either be different worksheets in a single file, or it may be preferable to break a system down into a number of smaller files that are subsequently linked together.

Positive aspects of this spreadsheet

The overall picture of revenue, costs and profits is clear. The spreadsheet has been designed in such a way that further enhancement will be relatively easy.

SPREADSHEET 10

An important aspect of spreadsheet design is to build into the system checks on the arithmetical accuracy. This might include validating input data through the use of an IF function, or performing a cross-check on a calculation.

One way of cross-checking a calculation is to create a control box. Such a box has been created for the plan used in this chapter and is shown in Figure 9.12.

	I	J	K	L	M	N	O
1							
2							
3			**Arithmetic Balance Check**				
4							
5							
6				**Control Box**			
7				*Profit and Loss Account*			
8							
9			Vertical Total		78383		
10			Horizontal Total		78383		
11			Difference		0		
12							

Figure 9.12 Cross-check control box

The logic required for the formulae in cells M9 and M10, which calculate the total net profit at the end of the year are:

SUM(B18..E18)

and

SUM(F9..F12)–F7–F16

A macro could also be created that alerts the user should the arithmetic not balance, probably by sounding a beep and going to a suitable message screen.

Problems with this spreadsheet

This simple technique only provides an arithmetic check. It is possible that the spreadsheet might be quite wrong for a number of other reasons, while arithmetically balancing.

Positive aspects of this spreadsheet

The control box provides an arithmetic check on the cross-addition of the rows and columns. It is easy to see if the spreadsheet balances by checking cell M11. This idea draws on the time honoured accounting concern of balancing financial statements. However, it is important to remember that even if the control box appears to balance it is still possible for the underlying logic of the plan to be wrong.

SPREADSHEET 11

It is useful to support the information supplied in business plans with charts. In the plan used here various charts might be useful, for example to show the relative impact of price and sales volume figures. Although charts can be placed on the same worksheet as the plan, it is usually preferable to keep graphs on separate *chart sheets*. The exception might be if it is appropriate to view changes on a chart at the same time data in the plan is changed, or if a worksheet is to be copied into a management report being created on a word processor. Figure 9.13 is an example of the type of chart that might be produced from the plan used in this chapter.

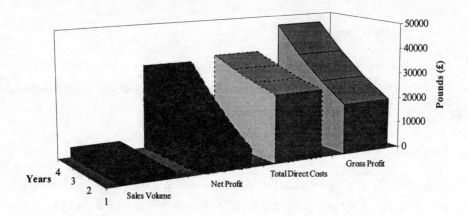

Figure 9.13 Three-dimensional graph

SPREADSHEET 12

The plan used in this chapter has been a simple quarterly plan, but in many cases plans will be much larger. Figure 9.14 is an extract from a five year quarterly plan. Although it is not obvious by looking at Figure 9.14, each year in this report has been formatted with a different colour font. This is a useful technique when working with large models because it enables the user to quickly know which part of the plan is being viewed or worked on, without having to scroll around the spreadsheet to see the titles. This colour coding can then be carried over to summary reports, and other reports pertaining to the different parts of the plan.

From a design point of view it is preferable to place different reports associated with a plan on separate worksheets. The report in Figure 9.15, which has been placed on a separate sheet called *Summary* is created by referencing the cells from the yearly totals in the main plan.

	A	B	C	D	E	F	G	H	I	J	K
1	Five Year Profit Projection for Widget Division for 1998										
2		Written by P.A. Jones 31 July 1997									
3											
4		Y1 Qtr 1	Y1 Qtr 2	Y1 Qtr 3	Y2 Qtr 4	Y1 Total	Y2 Qtr 1	Y2 Qtr 2	Y2 Qtr 3	Y2 Qtr 4	Y2 Total
5	Sales Volume	8000	8080	8161	8242	32483	12000	12000	12000	12000	48000
6	Price	50.00	50.75	51.61	52.28		67.00	67.00	67.00	67.00	
7	Revenue	400000	410060	420373	430945	1661378	804000	804000	804000	804000	3216000
8											
9	Raw Materials	96000	96960	97930	98909	389798	180000	180000	180000	180000	720000
10	Labour	12000	12060	12120	12181	48361	15000	15150	15302	15455	60906
11	Energy	9600	9792	9988	10186	39567	10000	10050	10100	10151	40301
12	Depreciation	2000	2020	2040	2061	8121	2500	2519	2538	2557	10113
13	Total Direct Costs	119600	120832	122078	123338	485843	207500	207719	207939	208162	831320
14											
15	Gross Profit	280400	289228	298295	307607	1175530	596500	596281	596061	595838	2384680
16	Overheads	20000	20300	20605	20914	81818	22000	22220	22442	22667	89329
17											
18	Net Profit	260400	268928	277691	286694	1093712	574500	574061	573618	573171	2295351

Figure 9.14 Five year extended plan

	A	B	C	D	E	F	G
1	Five Year Summary Profit Projection for Widget Division for 1998						
2		Written by P.A. Jones 31 July 1997					
3							
4		Y1 Total	Y2 Total	Y3 Total	Y4 Total	Y5 Total	5 yr Total
5	Sales Volume	32483	48000	60452	72542	90675	304152
6	Average Annual Price	51.14	67.00	70.97	71.06	71.06	
7	Revenue	1661378	3216000	4290334	5154924	6444709	20767344
8							
9	Raw Materials	389798	720000	1027676	1233211	1813508	5184192
10	Labour	48361	60906	64966	68000	70067	312301
11	Energy	39567	40301	40301	48361	113750	282281
12	Depreciation	8121	10113	10113	12090	12945	53382
13	Total Direct Costs	485848	831320	1143056	1361662	2010270	5832156
14							
15	Gross Profit	1175530	2384680	3147278	3793262	4434439	14935189
16	Overheads	81818	89329	89329	89329	97816	447621
17							
18	Net Profit	1093712	2295351	3057949	3703933	4336623	14487568

Figure 9.15 Summary report

LABOUR SAVING TEMPLATES

A business plan that requires time and effort to design and implement is likely to be in regular use for some time. In addition, the data in the plan will almost certainly change, either as situations change, or on a periodic basis. In this instance it is advisable to convert the developed plan into a template, into which different data can be entered whenever necessary.

A template is a fully developed plan from which the data has been removed, but the formulae remain. When new data is entered so the formulae will be calculated. Figure 9.16 shows the one year quarterly plan with the data removed and the input cells highlighted by shading the cells. The file can be found on the CD accompanying the book under the name **TEMPLAT1**.

When the input cells are set to zero all other cells that are directly or indirectly related to those cells should also display zero. The only exception to this is if there are division formulae in which case a division by zero error will be displayed. The act of removing the data is a useful auditing tool, because if values are found in any cells this indicates that there is an error in the way that the plan was developed which can be rectified.

When the template is complete the spreadsheet should be protected and then only the input cells unprotected in order that the user can only enter data into the designated cells. It is also important to save the file now as a Template file as opposed to a Worksheet file. This is achieved by selecting File Save As and then, in Excel selecting Template (*.XLT) in the File Type box, and in 1-2-3 selecting SmartMaster (WT4) in the File Type Box. In either case the file is then saved as a Template, or Master file. To use the template File New is selected which accesses the Template or Master directory and when a file is selected a copy of it is opened, leaving the original template unchanged on the disk.

	A	B	C	D	E	F
1		Qtr 1	Qtr 2	Qtr 3	Qtr 4	Total
2	Sales Volume	0	0	0	0	0
3	Price	0.00	0.00	0.00	0.00	
4	Revenue	0	0	0	0	0
5						
6	Raw Materials	0	0	0	0	0
7	Labour	0	0	0	0	0
8	Energy	0.00	0	0	0	0
9	Depreciation	0	0	0	0	0
10	Total Direct Costs	0	0	0	0	0
11						
12	Gross Profit	0	0	0	0	0
13	Overheads	0	0	0	0	0
14	Net Profit	0	0	0	0	0
15						
16	Growth factors					
17	Sales Volume	0.00%				
18	Price	0.00%				
19	Raw Materials	0.00%				
20	Labour	0.00%				
21	Energy	0.00%				
22	Depreciation	0.00%				
23	Overheads	0.00%				

Figure 9.16 Plan converted to a template

Data input forms

A further enhancement that makes working with templates easier to control is to remove all the data from the main plan and place it on one or more data input forms. Figure 9.17 is a data input form for the quarterly plan, and Figure 9.18 shows the amended formulae in the plan which picks up the data from the input form. The file, which has been named **TEMPLAT2** can be found on the CD accompanying the book.

	A	B	C
1	Profit Projection Input Form		
2	Written by P.A. Jones 31 July 1995		
3			
4	Input Variable	Opening value	Growth or cost factor
5	Sales Volume	0	0.00%
6	Price	0.00	0.00%
7			
8	Raw Material cost per unit	#N/A	0.00
9	Labour	0	0.00%
10	Energy	0	0.00%
11	Depreciation	0	0.00%
12			
13	Overheads	0	0.00%

Figure 9.17 Data input form

	A	B	C	D	E	F
1						
2						
3						
4		Qtr 1	Qtr 2	Qtr 3	Qtr 4	Total
5	Sales Volume	=Input!B5	=B5*(1+Input!$C$5)	=C5*(1+Input!$C$5)	=D5*(1+Input!$C$5)	=SUM(B5:E5)
6	Price	=Input!B6	=B6*(1+Input!$C$5)	=C6*(1+Input!$C$5)	=D6*(1+Input!$C$5)	
7	Revenue	=B5*B6	=C5*C6	=D5*D6	=E5*E6	=SUM(B7:E7)
8						
9	Raw Materials	=P&L!B5*Input!$C$8	=P&L!C5*Input!$C$8	=P&L!D5*Input!$C$8	=P&L!E5*Input!$C$8	=SUM(B9:E9)
10	Labour	=Input!B9	=B10*(1+Input!$C$9)	=C10*(1+Input!$C$9)	=D10*(1+Input!$C$9)	=SUM(B10:E10)
11	Energy	=Input!B10	=B11*(1+Input!$C$10)	=C11*(1+Input!$C$10)	=D11*(1+Input!$C$10)	=SUM(B11:E11)
12	Depreciation	=Input!B11	=B12*(1+Input!$C$11)	=C12*(1+Input!$C$11)	=D12*(1+Input!$C$11)	=SUM(B12:E12)
13	Total Direct Costs	=SUM(B9:B12)	=SUM(C9:C12)	=SUM(D9:D12)	=SUM(E9:E12)	=SUM(F9:F12)
14						
15	Gross Profit	=B7-B13	=C7-C13	=D7-D13	=E7-E13	=SUM(B15:E15)
16	Overheads	=Input!B13	=B16*(1+Input!$C$13)	=C16*(1+Input!$C$13)	=D16*(1+Input!$C$13)	=SUM(B16:E16)
17						
18	Net Profit	=B15-B16	=C15-C16	=D15-D16	=E15-E16	=SUM(B18:E18)

Figure 9.18 Amended formulae to reference data input form

There are many benefits to be derived from using data input forms including the fact that the data can be checked more easily. Sometimes it might be possible to design an input form that is compatible with a forecasting or accounting system so that the data can be electronically picked up from the other system without having to type it in again. It also means that the spreadsheet containing all the logic for the plan can be protected, and if necessary made read-only, in order to maintain the integrity of the system.

It is not a trivial task to change existing systems to be templates with data input forms, Furthermore, it will also take a little longer to develop a new system in this way, as opposed to incorporating the data with the logic. However, the ease of data input and ongoing maintenance should make the additional effort worthwhile.

SUMMARY

This chapter has considered some of the principal design elements that should be considered when embarking on the creation of any business model or plan, be it a financial statement, a budgetary control system, a marketing model or a forecasting plan. A small plan has been used for demonstration purposes, and many of the techniques become essential with larger plans. Taking time to consider the layout and design of a system before embarking on its development has been proven by many users to pay considerable dividends in the long term. In addition it is worth talking with colleagues who might find a plan useful before starting development to see whether some additional lines might need to be incorporated, as it is always more difficult to add to a spreadsheet later.

Developing a Financial Plan

Planning unifies diverse activities, providing a 'road map' for the undertaking of complete tasks that must be well co-ordinated, accomplished over extended time frames and inclusive of many people.

R. K. Wysocki and J. Young, *Information Systems – Management Principles in Action*, Singapore, John Wiley & Sons Inc., 1990.

INTRODUCTION

Financial planning is one of the most popular spreadsheet applications. It involves acquiring a sales forecast, perhaps using one of the models or methods described in Part One of this book, and then specifying all the resources necessary to ensure that the forecast targets are reached. Financial planning may be performed for the firm as a whole, or at departmental or divisional level. When separate divisional profit plans are developed they will usually need to be subsequently incorporated into a corporate plan.

The model

The financial plan described here is a one year quarterly plan for a manufacturing company. It is a deterministic plan and assumes point estimates for the opening input values, as well as the growth and cost factors. In this example all growth rates and cost factors remain the same for the duration of the plan. The completed model can be found on the CD accompanying this book under the name **FINPLAN**.

The plan consists of six separate worksheets. The first is a Data Input sheet. For this example all the input data has been grouped onto one sheet, but in some situations, if there is a large amount of input, it might be preferable to break the input down into multiple sheets. The second worksheet is a Profit and Loss Account that shows how the firms' income will be made and what costs will be incurred in generating this income. The Profit and Loss Appropriation Account, which provides an estimate of tax payable, the dividends payable, and the funds to be transferred to reserve accounts for future growth is also on this worksheet.

The third worksheet is a Balance Sheet, followed by Funds Flow Statement, some Ratio Analysis, and finally a Cash Flow Statement.

Getting started

The first step when creating a multi-sheet plan such as this is to collect as much information as possible in terms of the line items, variables, growth and cost factors, etc., and then to name worksheets and enter titles, column headings and line item descriptions. This forms the basic structure of the plan and makes cross-sheet referencing possible when formulae are developed. Figures 10.1 through 10.6 show the six worksheets that make up the full plan with sample data.

The worksheets have been named as follow: *Input, P&L, Balsheet, Funds Flow, Ratios* and *Cash Flow*. These names will be referenced by formulae when cross-sheet references are required.

	A	B	C	D	E	F
1	**Input Area for all parts**					
2						
3	**Profit and Loss Account**					
4		*Opening Figs*	*Growth*	*Open Prop*	*Base Variable*	
5	Volume	6000	3.00%			
6	Unit Price	10	2.00%			
7	Materials per Unit	4				
8	Labour	10000	1.50%			
9	Energy	8000	2.00%			
10	Administration			2.50%	of turnover	
11	Depreciation	1500				
12	Finance Charges	1200				
13	Maintenance			0.01	per unit	
14	Salaries	13000	6.00%			
15						
16	Corporate Tax Rate	30.00%				
17						
18	**Profit and Loss Appropriation Account**					
19		*1 qtr*	*2 qtr*	*3 qtr*	*4 qtr*	
20	Dividends	0	2100	0	2100	
21	Reserves	0	0	0	3500	
22						
23	**Balance Sheet**					
24	ASSETS					
25	Fixed assets	*Opening Bal*				
26	Land & Building	45000				
27	Plant & Equipment	26500				
28	Fixtures & Fittings	4500				
29	Motor Vehicles	7500				
30	Depreciation	15000				
31						
32	Current assets	*Opening Bal*				
33	Inventory	39500				
34	Debtors	67000				
35	Prepayments	1000				
36	Cash	24000				
37						
38						
39	CAPITAL					
40		*Opening Bal*				
41	Share capital	75000				
42	Retained profit	9250				
43	Reserves	5500				
44						
45	LIABILITIES					
46	Long term liabilities	*Opening Bal*				
47	Debenture	20000				
48	Loan	25250				
49	Mortgage	30500				
50						
51	Current Liabilities	*Opening Bal*				
52	Trade creditors	30500				
53	Tax	2500				
54	Dividends	1500				
55						
56		*Opening Bal*				
57	Previous periods sales	36500				

Figure 10.1 Data Input worksheet (*Input)*

	A	B	C	D	E	F	G
1	**Final Accounts Template**						
2							
3	**Profit & Loss Account**		*1st qtr.*	*2nd qtr.*	*3rd qtr.*	*4th qtr.*	*Total*
4	Volume		6000	6180	6365	6556	25102
5	Unit price		10.00	10.20	10.40	10.61	
6	**Turnover**		60000	63036	66226	69577	258838
7							
8	Materials		24000	24720	25462	26225	100407
9	Labour		10000	10150	10302	10457	40909
10	Energy		8000	8160	8323	8490	32973
11	**Total direct costs**		42000	43030	44087	45172	174289
12							
13	**Gross Profit**		18000	20006	22139	24405	84549
14							
15	Administration		1500	1576	1656	1739	6471
16	Depreciation		1500	1500	1500	1500	6000
17	Finance charges		1200	1200	1200	1200	4800
18	Maintenance		600	630	662	696	2588
19	Salaries		13000	13780	14607	15483	56870
20	**Total other costs**		17800	18686	19625	20618	76729
21							
22	**Net Profit B.T.**		200	1320	2514	3786	7820
23							
24	Provision for tax		60	396	754	1136	2346
25	**Net Profit A.T.**		140	924	1760	2650	5474
26	**Cumulative profit**		140	1064	2824	5474	
27							
28	Dividends		0	2100	0	2100	4200
29	Reserves		0	0	0	3500	3500
30	Cumulative apportionments		0	2100	2100	7700	7700
31	**Retained Profit**		140	-1176	1760	-2950	

Figure 10.2 Profit and Loss Account worksheet (*P&L*)

	A	B	C	D	E	F
1	**Balance Sheet at 31 December 2XXX**					
2						
3	**ASSETS**					
4	**Fixed assets**	*Opening Bal*	*1st qtr.*	*2nd qtr.*	*3rd qtr.*	*4th qtr.*
5	Land & Building	45000	45000	45000	45000	45000
6	Plant & Equipment	26500	26500	26500	26500	26500
7	Fixtures & Fittings	4500	4500	4500	4500	4500
8	Motor Vehicles	7500	7500	7500	7500	7500
9	Depreciation	15000	16500	18000	19500	21000
10	**Total net fixed assets**	68500	67000	65500	64000	62500
11						
12	**Current assets**	*Opening Bal*	*1st qtr.*	*2nd qtr.*	*3rd qtr.*	*4th qtr.*
13	Inventory	39500	39500	39500	39500	39500
14	Debtors	67000	60000	63036	66226	69577
15	Prepayments	1000	1000	1000	1000	1000
16	Cash	24000	37500	38270	40111	43094
17	**Total current assets**	131500	138000	141806	146836	153170
18						
19	**Current Liabilities**					
20	Trade creditors	30500	35300	36286	37303	38350
21	Tax	2500	2560	2956	3710	4846
22	Dividends	1500	1500	3600	3600	5700
23	**Total Current Liabilities**	34500	39360	42842	44613	48896
24						
25	Working Capital	97000	98640	98964	102224	104274
26	**Total assets**	165500	165640	164464	166224	166774
27						
28	**Long term liabilities**					
29	Debenture	20000	20000	20000	20000	20000
30	Loan	25250	25250	25250	25250	25250
31	Mortgage	30500	30500	30500	30500	30500
32	**Total long term liabilities**	75750	75750	75750	75750	75750
33						
34	**Total net assets**	89750	89890	88714	90474	91024
35						
36	**CAPITAL**					
37		*Opening Bal*	*1st qtr.*	*2nd qtr.*	*3rd qtr.*	*4th qtr.*
38	Share capital	75000	75000	75000	75000	75000
39	Retained profit	9250	9390	8214	9974	7024
40	Reserves	5500	5500	5500	5500	9000
41	**Owners equity**	89750	89890	88714	90474	91024
42						
43	**Total Capital & Liabilities**	165500	165640	164464	166224	166774

Figure 10.3 Balance Sheet worksheet (*Balsheet*)

	A	B	C	D	E	F
1	**Funds Flow Statement**					
2						
3	**ASSETS**					
4	**Fixed assets**			*2nd qtr.*	*3rd qtr.*	*4th qtr.*
5	Land & Building			0	0	0
6	Plant & Equipment			0	0	0
7	Fixtures & Fittings			0	0	0
8	Motor Vehicles			0	0	0
9	Depreciation			1500	1500	1500
10	**Total net fixed assets**			-1500	-1500	-1500
11						
12	**Current assets**					
13	Inventory			0	0	0
14	Debtors			3036	3190	3351
15	Prepayments			0	0	0
16	Cash			770	1841	2983
17	**Total current assets**			3806	5030	6334
18						
19	**Current Liabilities**					
20	Trade creditors			986	1016	1048
21	Tax			396	754	1136
22	Dividends			2100	0	2100
23	**Total Current Liabilities**			3482	1771	4284
24						
25	Working Capital			324	3260	2050
26	**Total Assets**			-1176	1760	550
27						
28	**Long term liabilities**					
29	Debenture			0	0	0
30	Loan			0	0	0
31	Mortgage			0	0	0
32	**Total long term liabilities**			0	0	0
33						
34	**Total net assets**			-1176	1760	550
35						
36	**CAPITAL**					
37				*2nd qtr.*	*3rd qtr.*	*4th qtr.*
38	Share capital			0	0	0
39	Retained profit			-1176	1760	-2950
40	Reserves			0	0	3500
41	**Owners equity**			-1176	1760	550
42						
43	**Total Capital & Liabilities**			-1176	1760	550

Figure 10.4 Funds Flow worksheet (*Funds Flow*)

	A	B	C	D	E	F
1	**Ratio Analysis**					
2			*1st qtr.*	*2nd qtr.*	*3rd qtr.*	*4th qtr.*
3	Current ratio		3.51	3.31	3.29	3.13
4	Quick ratio		2.50	2.39	2.41	2.32
5	Equity to debt		0.78	0.75	0.75	0.73
6	Gross profit %		30.00%	31.74%	33.43%	35.08%
7	Net profit %		0.33%	2.09%	3.80%	5.44%
8	Materials to turnover %		40.00%	39.22%	38.45%	37.69%
9	Labour to turnover %		16.67%	16.10%	15.56%	15.03%
10	Energy to turnover %		13.33%	12.94%	12.57%	12.20%
11	Administration to turnover %		2.50%	2.50%	2.50%	2.50%
12	Depreciation to turnover %		2.50%	2.38%	2.26%	2.16%
13	Finance charges to turnover %		2.00%	1.90%	1.81%	1.72%
14	Maintenance to turnover %		1.00%	1.00%	1.00%	1.00%
15	Salaries to turnover %		21.67%	21.86%	22.06%	22.25%
16	Stock turnover		6.08	6.38	6.71	7.05
17	No. of days in inventory		60	57	54	52
18	Asset turnover		1.45	1.53	1.59	1.67
19	Capital output		0.69	0.65	0.63	0.60
20	Net working capital		98640	98964	102224	104274
21	Working capital turnover		2.43	2.55	2.59	2.67
22	No. of days debtors		91	91	91	91
23	No. of days creditors		88	88	88	88
24	Return on investment		0.48%	3.21%	6.05%	9.08%
25	Return on equity		0.62%	4.17%	7.78%	11.65%

Figure 10.5 Ratio Analysis worksheet (*Ratios*)

	A	B	C	D	E	F
1	**Cash flow plan**					
2			*1st qtr.*	*2nd qtr.*	*3rd qtr.*	*4th qtr.*
3	Opening Cash Balance		24000	37500	38270	40111
4						
5	*Cash in*					
6	Sales from previous period		36500	60000	63036	66226
7	Investments		0	0	0	0
8	Other cash receipts		0	0	0	0
9						
10	*Cash out*					
11	Cash expenses		23000	23930	24909	25940
12	Creditors		30500	35300	36286	37303
13	Tax paid		0	0	0	0
14	Dividends paid		0	0	0	0
15	**Balance**		7000	38270	40111	43094
16	**Cum Balance**		7000	45270	85381	128474

Figure 10.6 Cash Flow Statement worksheet (*Cash Flow*)

Developing the Profit and Loss Account

The data input sheet in Figure 10.1 shows all the assumptions that have been made for the Profit and Loss Account. For example the sales volume begins at 6000 and increases by 6% per period, the unit price begins at 10 and increases at 2%, the cost of raw materials is £4 per unit, etc.

Having prepared the structure for this part of the plan the logic can now be entered. The opening sales volume value is required in cell C4 of the *P&L* sheet and therefore a reference to the *Input* sheet, cell B5 is entered as follows:

Input!$B$5

In the second and subsequent periods the sales volume is to grow by the value entered in cell C5 of the *Input* sheet. The following formula is therefore required in cell D4 of the *P&L* sheet:

C4*(1+Input!$C$5)

This formula can then be extrapolated for the remaining two quarters. Note that the use of the absolute reference ensures that the reference to cell C5 in the *Input* sheet remains fixed.

The total sales volume in cell G4 of the *P&L* sheet is calculated with the SUM function as follows:

SUM(C4:F4)

The remaining lines in the Profit and Loss Account follow the same principles and Figure 10.8 shows the formulae for this part of the financial plan.

	A	B	C	D	E	F	G
3	Profit & Loss Ac		1st qtr.	2nd qtr.	3rd qtr.	4th qtr.	Total
4	Volume		=Input!$B$5	=C4*(1+Input!$C$5)	=D4*(1+Input!$C$5)	=E4*(1+Input!$C$5)	=SUM(C4:F4)
5	Unit price		=Input!$B$6	=C5*(1+Input!$C$6)	=D5*(1+Input!$C$6)	=E5*(1+Input!$C$6)	
6	Turnover		=C4*C5	=D4*D5	=E4*E5	=F4*F5	=SUM(C6:F6)
7							
8	Materials		=C4*Input!$B$7	=D4*Input!$B$7	=E4*Input!$B$7	=F4*Input!$B$7	=SUM(C8:F8)
9	Labour		=Input!$B$8	=C9*(1+Input!$C$8)	=D9*(1+Input!$C$8)	=E9*(1+Input!$C$8)	=SUM(C9:F9)
10	Energy		=Input!$B$9	=C10*(1+Input!$C$9)	=D10*(1+Input!$C$9)	=E10*(1+Input!$C$9)	=SUM(C10:F10)
11	Total direct costs		=SUM(C8:C10)	=SUM(D8:D10)	=SUM(E8:E10)	=SUM(F8:F10)	=SUM(G8:G10)
12							
13	Gross Profit		=C6-C11	=D6-D11	=E6-E11	=F6-F11	=G6-G11
14							
15	Administration		=C6*Input!$D$10	=D6*Input!$D$10	=E6*Input!$D$10	=F6*Input!$D$10	=SUM(C15:F15)
16	Depreciation		=Input!$B$11	=C16	=D16	=E16	=SUM(C16:F16)
17	Finance charges		=Input!$B$12	=C17	=D17	=E17	=SUM(C17:F17)
18	Maintenance		=C6*Input!$D$13	=D6*Input!$D$13	=E6*Input!$D$13	=F6*Input!$D$13	=SUM(C18:F18)
19	Salaries		=Input!$B$14	=C19*(1+Input!$C$14)	=D19*(1+Input!$C$14)	=E19*(1+Input!$C$14)	=SUM(C19:F19)
20	Total other costs		=SUM(C15:C19)	=SUM(D15:D19)	=SUM(E15:E19)	=SUM(F15:F19)	=SUM(G15:G19)
21							
22	Net Profit B.T.		=C13-C20	=D13-D20	=E13-E20	=F13-F20	=G13-G20
23							
24	Provision for tax		=C22*Input!$B$16	=D22*Input!$B$16	=E22*Input!$B$16	=F22*Input!$B$16	=SUM(C24:F24)
25	Net Profit A.T.		=C22-C24	=D22-D24	=E22-E24	=F22-F24	=SUM(C25:F25)
26	Cumulative profit		=C25+B26	=D25+C26	=E25+D26	=F25+E26	

Figure 10.8 Formulae for Profit and Loss Account

Developing the profit and loss appropriation account

The assumptions for the profit and loss appropriation account are again entered on the *Input* sheet and they involve the dividends and reserves. As these values can change for each period the lines on the *Input* sheet have allowed for four different values to be entered. In this example dividends of 2100 have been entered in the 2nd and 4th quarters and reserves of 3500 have been entered in the 4th quarter.

The lines in the Appropriation Account on the *P&L* sheet need to refer to the appropriate cells on the *Input* sheet. Figure 10.9 shows the formulae required for this part of the financial plan.

	A	B	C	D	E	F	G
26	Cumulative profit		=C25+B26	=D25+C26	=E25+D26	=F25+E26	
27							
28	Dividends		=Input!B20	=Input!C20	=Input!D20	=Input!E20	=SUM(C28:F28)
29	Reserves		=Input!B21	=Input!C21	=Input!D21	=Input!E21	=SUM(C29:F29)
30	Cumulative apportionments		=C28+C29	=C30+D28+D29	=D30+E28+E29	=E30+F28+F29	=F30
31	Retained Profit		=C26-C30	=D26-D28-D29	=E26-E28-E29	=F26-F28-F29	
32							

Figure 10.9 Formulae for P&L Appropriation Account

Developing the balance sheet

The balance sheet has been developed following the North–South convention, which means that the assets and liabilities are placed in what amounts to a vertical column. This is the more usual convention today with the more traditional, or old-fashioned East–West convention, where the assets and liabilities are placed side by side, being much less frequently used.

Assets

The opening balances and the assumptions with regards debtors and creditors are again found on the *Input* sheet. The assumptions made for the debtors and creditors in the balance sheet are that they are paid in full in the following period. The only cash payments made are the labour and salary costs.

The fixed assets and the current assets are taken from the *Input* sheet and do not change over the four quarters of the Balance Sheet. The Depreciation in the first quarter is calculated by multiplying the opening balance by the Depreciation value for the first quarter in the *P&L* sheet. This formula can then be copied for the remaining periods.

The debtors are calculated by taking the turnover for the current period.

The logic for the cash calculation in the first quarter is as follows:

(Opening cash balance – Labour – Salaries) + Previous periods' sales)

Therefore, the formula required in cell C16 of the *Balsheet* sheet is:

(B16–'P&L'!C9–'P&L'!C19)+Input!B57

Unfortunately it is not possible to simply extrapolate this formula for the remaining quarters because in the second quarter it is necessary to incorporate the turnover for the first quarter less the trade creditors. Therefore the formula required in cell D16 is:

(C16–'P&L'!D9-'P&L'!D19)+'P&L'!C6-C20

The formula in cell D16 can then be copied to the fourth quarter in cell F16.

Capital and liabilities

The current liabilities consist of the trade creditors, tax and dividends. The opening balance for the trade creditors is taken from the *Input* sheet, but in the first quarter the creditors are calculated by taking the total direct costs less the labour (which is paid in cash) plus the total other costs less the salaries and depreciation. Therefore the formula required in cell C20, which can be copied for the remaining periods is:

'P&L'!C11–'P&L'!C9+'P&L'!C20-'P&L'!C19–'P&L'!C16

The opening tax and the dividends are both taken from the *Input* sheet and in the first quarter the opening values are added to the provision for tax made and the dividends respectively in the profit and loss account. Therefore the formulae required in cells C20 and C21, which can be copied for the remaining periods are:

B21+'P&L'!C24
and
B22+'P&L'!C28

The working capital is the total current assets less the total current liabilities and therefore the formula required in cell B25, which can be copied for the remaining periods is:

=B17–B23

The long-term liabilities consist of debenture, loan and mortgage payments, which are all taken from the *Input* sheet and remain the same for the year.

The total net assets are the total assets less the total long-term liabilities and therefore the formula required in cell B34, which can be copied for the remaining periods is:

=B26–B32

Capital consist of share capital, retained profit and reserves. Share capital is taken from the *Input* sheet and carried across for the four quarters. The opening retained profit is also taken from the *Input* sheet, but in the first quarter the retained profit from the first quarter of the profit and loss account is included. Therefore the formula required in cell C39 which can be copied for the remaining periods is:

B39+'P&L'!C31

The same procedure is required for the reserves by picking up the opening reserves from the balance sheet section of the *Input* sheet and then adding in the reserves from the profit and loss account in the subsequent quarters.

The total capital and liabilities can then be calculated by adding together the total net assets and the owners' equity. Therefore the formula required in cell B43, which can be copied for the remaining periods is:

B41+B32

Funds flow statement

The funds flow statement is a tool for understanding how funds are being used in the organisation. It indicates into which assets money is being invested or disinvested as well as showing how these funds have been financed or which sources of finance are being repaid.

The statement of source and application of funds is calculated by subtracting two consecutive balance sheets from each other. This will then indicate which assets are increasing or decreasing, and which sources of funds are being used or being paid back.

The layout of a funds flow statement differs from country to country and company to company and the following shows the principles of how to set up a statement, but readers will need to format the final report to suit individual requirements.

The basic statement can be quickly created on the spreadsheet by copying the headings and titles from the balance sheet (*Balsheet)* onto the *Funds Flow* sheet. The first column of the source and application of funds statement will represent the second quarter, being the first quarter values from the balance sheet less the opening balance, and thus the titles for the opening balance and the first quarter can be deleted. The following formula can then be entered into cell D5:

BalSheet!D5–BalSheet!C5

This formula can be copied for all the remaining cells in the statement.

Ratio analysis

There are many different ratios that can be applied to a financial statement and Figure 10.6 shows a selection that have been calculated on the *Ratios* sheet. Figure 10.10 shows the formulae for the first quarter ratios which have been copied for the remaining periods.

	A	B	C
1	**Ratio Analysis**		
2			*1st qtr.*
3	Current ratio		=BalSheet!C17/BalSheet!C23
4	Quick ratio		=SUM(BalSheet!C14:C16)/BalSheet!C23
5	Equity to debt		=BalSheet!C41/(BalSheet!C32+BalSheet!C23)
6	Gross profit %		='P&L'!C13/'P&L'!C6
7	Net profit %		='P&L'!C22/'P&L'!C6
8	Materials to turnover %		='P&L'!C8/'P&L'!C6
9	Labour to turnover %		='P&L'!C9/'P&L'!C6
10	Energy to turnover %		='P&L'!C10/'P&L'!C6
11	Administration to turnover %		='P&L'!C15/'P&L'!C6
12	Depreciation to turnover %		='P&L'!C16/'P&L'!C6
13	Finance charges to turnover %		='P&L'!C17/'P&L'!C6
14	Maintenance to turnover %		='P&L'!C18/'P&L'!C6
15	Salaries to turnover %		='P&L'!C19/'P&L'!C6
16	Stock turnover		='P&L'!C6/BalSheet!C13*4
17	No. of days in inventory		=BalSheet!C13/('P&L'!C6*4)*365
18	Asset turnover		='P&L'!C6/BalSheet!C26*4
19	Capital output		=1/C18
20	Net working capital		=BalSheet!C17-BalSheet!C23
21	Working capital turnover		='P&L'!C6/Ratios!C20*4
22	No. of days debtors		=BalSheet!C14/('P&L'!C6*4)*365
23	No. of days creditors		=('P&L'!C8+'P&L'!C10+'P&L'!C15+'P&L'!C18)/BalSheet!C20*365/4
24	Return on investment		='P&L'!C22/BalSheet!C26*4
25	Return on equity		='P&L'!C25/BalSheet!C41*4

Figure 10.9 Formulae for ratio analysis

Cash flow statement

Traditional financial statements produced by an organisation are essentially historic in nature. They show what assets have been acquired and how they have been funded, as well as showing what income has been made and how it has been dispersed. Although all this information is considerable value to management, it does suffer from this strong historical perspective. To counter this, organisations developed techniques of forecasting, planning and budgeting and one of the most important tools available to management is the cash flow plan.

The cash flow plan shows what money the organisation expects to receive and from what sources as well as how it intends to spend it.

The cash balance row of the cash flow plan is the same as the cash row of the balance sheet and therefore the formula in cell C3 that is copied for the remaining periods is:

BalSheet!B16

The cash-in section includes sales, investments and cash receipts. In this example there are no investments to be considered and no payments are received in cash, but the sales is the turnover from the previous period. Therefore the opening sales is a reference to the opening sales in the *Input* sheet:

Input!B57

In the following period the sales from the profit and loss account in cell C6 can be referenced and this can then be copied for the remaining periods.

The cash-out section of the cash flow plan includes the cash expenses, the creditors and repayments. The cash expenses include labour and salaries which means the following formula is required in cell C11 and can be copied for the remaining periods.

'P&L'!C9+'P&L'!C19

The opening creditors in cell C12 can be picked up from Cell B20 in the balance sheet and the reference can be copied for the remaining periods.

There are no tax or dividend payments, although accommodation for these has been included in the cash flow plan. The cash balance can finally be calculated by taking the opening cash balance, adding the total cash in and subtracting the total cash out. Therefore the formula required in cell C15, which can be copied for the remaining periods is:

C3+SUM(C6:C8)–SUM(C11:C14)

SUMMARY

Having spent a considerable amount of time and effort developing an integrated financial statement such as the one described here, it is likely that it will be used periodically with different data. Because the input has been held separately on the *Input* sheet it is not difficult to convert this plan into a template. This involves removing all the data in the *Input* sheet, or entering zeros into the cells, which will cause the formulae in the other worksheets to return zero results, (with the exception of the *Ratios* sheet which will return division by zero errors). The file can then be saved as an XLT or WKT template file. The section on templates in Chapter 9 gives more details on how to do this.

Some Business Plans

A plan ... is 'tangible evidence of the thinking of management.' It results from planning.

J. O. McKinsey quoted by G. A. Steiner in *Top Management Planning*, Macmillan, New York, 1969.

INTRODUCTION

This chapter consists of a selection of different business plans that illustrate a range of spreadsheet techniques which readers may find helpful when developing their own systems. The business applications that have been selected for discussion in this chapter represent only a small number of the possible business spreadsheet applications and the areas chosen are:

- capital investment appraisal;
- break-even point analysis;
- learning curve costing;
- economic order quantity;
- sales campaign analysis.

For each of these examples the spreadsheet development approach and the key formulae are explained in detail in this chapter. However it is strongly recommended that readers study these plans in conjunction with the accompanying CD.

CAPITAL INVESTMENT APPRAISAL

The Capital Investment Appraisal (CIA) model described in this chapter uses both discounted and non-discounted techniques.

Discounted techniques are based on the time value of money. By this is meant that cash received today is more valuable than cash received at future dates. The rationale of this assertion is that cash can be invested as soon as it is received and thus immediately begin earning a return. Therefore the longer it takes to receive a sum of money, the less value that sum represents in today's terms.

Discounting techniques for capital investment appraisal reduce amounts paid and received in the future to the equivalent amount paid and received today. This is achieved through the application of the following formula that is multiplied by the sum of money concerned:

$$1/((1+I)^n)$$

where I = discount rate and n = number of periods in the future.

There are several *Discounted Cash Flow* (DCF) measures available in the spreadsheet, with the *Net Present Value* (NPV), the *Profitability Index* (PI) and the *Internal Rate of Return* (IRR) being some of the most frequently used.

The capital investment appraisal plan shown here calculates the NPV and the PI for both a fixed discount rate (FDR) and for a variable or inflation adjusted discount rate (VDR). Non-discounted cash flow measures of payback and rate of return are also produced.

The results of the FDR and VDR calculations are presented in such a way that the investment measures dependent on a discount rate can be compared and the difference between a fixed and variable discount rate on the NPV and PI can be evaluated. The model can be found on the CD accompanying this book under the name CIA.

Net present value

The purpose of the NPV is to calculate the balance between the *trade-off* in investment outlays and *future benefits* in terms of time-adjusted present monetary values. Thus the formula for NPV is:

NPV = Present value of cash flow in – present value of investment

NPV is a straightforward way of establishing whether, during the economic life of a project, a minimum earnings standard can be obtained.

The NPV may be defined as the difference between the sum of the values of the cash-in flows, discounted at an appropriate cost of capital, and the present value of the original investment. Provided the NPV is greater than or equal to zero the investment will earn the firm's required rate of return. The size of the NPV may be considered as either a measure of the surplus which the investment makes over its required return, or as the margin of error which may be made in the estimate of the investment amount before the investment will be rejected.

The interpretation of the NPV should be based on the following rules:

If NPV >= 0 then invest
If NPV < 0 then do not invest

Profitability index

The PI is defined as the sum of the present values of the cash-in flows divided by the present value of the investment. This produces a rate of return expressed as the number of discounted pounds and pence, or dollars and cents, or any other currency, that the investment will earn for every pound originally invested. The formula for the PI is:

$$PI = \frac{\sum \text{Present value of benefits}}{\text{Present value of investment}}$$

Internal rate of return

The IRR is the rate of interest which will cause the NPV to be zero. It is the internally generated return that the investment will earn throughout its life. It is also sometimes referred to as the *yield* of the investment. The formula for the IRR is:

IRR = i such that NPV = 0

The internal rate of return is the most complex of the three discounted cash flow statistical measures described here and it needs to be used with care. The internal rate of return may produce incorrect results if the investment shows negative cash flows after the first year of the project.

Developing a capital investment appraisal plan

Figure 11.1 shows the completed capital investment appraisal plan with some sample data.

	A	B	C	D	E	F	G
1	Capital Investment Appraisal System						
2			Cash-Out	Cash-In	Net Cash Movement each year		
3	IT Investment - Cash Out		350000		-350000		
4	Net Benefits	Year 1		60000	60000		
5		Year 2		95000	95000		
6		Year 3		120000	120000		
7		Year 4		180000	180000		
8		Year 5		200000	200000		
9	Fixed Cost of Capital or Interest Rate	20.00%					
10		Y1	Y2	Y3	Y4	Y5	
11	Estimated inflation rates	3.00%	4.00%	4.00%	3.00%	2.00%	
12							
13	Investment Reports for proposed investment						
14	Payback in years & months	3 years		5 months			
15	Discounted Payback FDR in years & months	4 years		11 months			
16	Rate of return(%)	37.43%					
17	NPV Fixed Discount Rate (FDR)	2598					
18	Profitability Index FDR (PI)	1.01					
19	Internal Rate of Return (IRR)	20.28%					
20							
21	Variable Discount Rates						
22	NPV Variable Discount Rates (VDR)	-115523					
23	Profitability Index VDR (PI)	0.67					

Figure 11.1 Capital investment appraisal plan

The investment reports

The investment reports consist of the simple payback and discounted payback in years and months, the rate of return, the NPV, the PI and the IRR at a fixed discount rate, as well as the payback, NPV and the PI at a variable discount rate.

Some of these reports can be calculated using built-in spreadsheet functions, but some, such as the payback and the variable discount rate reports require some additional calculations that have been grouped together in a separate area of the spreadsheet. Figure 11.2 shows the work area for the payback calculations.

	A	B	C	D	E	F	G
25	Payback work area						
26	Year no.	1	2	3	4	5	
27	Incomes	60000	95000	120000	180000	200000	
28	Cum Cash	60000	155000	275000	455000	655000	
29	Year no.	1	2	3	4	5	
30							
31	Amount after		3 years	275000			
32	Amount remaining			75000			
33	Value payable in following year			180000			
34	Part of year for remaining amount			5 months			
35							
36	Discounted payback work area						
37	Fixed Rate of Interest	20.00%					
38	Year no.	1	2	3	4	5	
39	Cash-Flow	60000	95000	120000	180000	200000	
40	DCF of cash-in	50000	65972	69444	86806	80376	
41	Cumulative DCF	50000	115972	185417	272222	352598	
42	Year no.	1	2	3	4	5	
43							
44	Amount after		4 years	272222			
45	Amount remaining			77778			
46	Value payable in following year			80376			
47	Part of year for remaining amount			11 months			

Figure 11.2 Payback work areas

Simple payback

The simple payback refers to the amount of time it takes for the original investment to be paid back in nominal terms.

Rows 25 through 28 is a lookup table from which the data for the simple payback is derived. The reason for repeating the year numbers will become clear shortly, but is to do with how the HLOOKUP function operates.

The formulae in the range B30 through D33 could be combined into a single, nested formula. However it is preferable to avoid long complex formulae and to break an operation down into a number of smaller modules. This makes auditing and amending the formula much easier.

The first step in calculating the payback is to ascertain the year in which the payback occurs in cell B30. The HLOOKUP function is used. This function requires three pieces of information.

1. what is to be looked up, which in this case it is the amount invested in cell C3;
2. the location of the lookup table, which is B27 through F28. The system will then look for the value in C3 across the first row of the specified table range. If an exact match cannot be found it will pick up the next lowest value. For this function to work properly in this context it is necessary for the values in the first row of the table to be sorted in ascending order;
3. the number of rows to offset for the result. This is slightly different for Excel and 1-2-3 because Excel counts the first row as 1, whereas 1-2-3 sees the first row as row 0.

The following is the formula required for cell B30.

In Excel:

=HLOOKUP(C3,B27:F28,2)

In 1-2-3:

@HLOOKUP(C3,B27...F28,1)

Given the data in the plan this formula will lookup 350000 in the first row of the table range B27 though F28 and, not finding an exact match, will find 275000 as the next lowest, coming down 1 row in the table will return 3 as the result. In other words payback is received in year 3.

In order to ascertain which month in year 3 payback occurs, it is necessary to know how much money was received by year 3. The following formula is required in cell D30:

In Excel:

=HLOOKUP(B30,B25:F27,3)

In 1-2-3:

@HLOOKUP(B30,B25...F27,2)

This formula looks up the value 3 in the table range B25 through F27 and then returns the value 2 rows down which is 275000.

The amount of money outstanding is calculated in cell D31 by subtracting the value in cell D30 from the investment in cell C3 which in this example is 75000.

To be able to calculate what proportion of a year this represents the amount of cash due in year 4 must be calculated, as follows:

In Excel:

=HLOOKUP(B30+1,B25:F28,2)

In 1-2-3:

@HLOOKUP(B30+1,B25...F28,1)

This produces a result of 180000. The number of months can then be calculated by dividing 75000 by 180000 and multiplying by 12 in cell D33 as follows:

D31/D32*12

The calculation of the payback is a good example of when a substantial amount of work is required to calculate something that can be visually calculated quite easily just by looking at the data on the screen. However, to ensure that an up-to-date payback is always reported the logic must be built-in to the plan.

Discounted payback

The simple payback as described above is regarded as not being an adequate measure of investment performance because it does not take into account the time value of money. The discounted payback, which is calculated after the future cash flows have been discounted, is regarded as a much stronger indication of the realistic period which is required to recover the investment. This calculation requires each cash flow to be individually discounted and the new discounted values are then used in the same way as was shown in the simple payback. The formula required for the discounted cash flow in row 39 of Figure 11.2 is as follows:

B38/(1+$B$36)^B37

Rate of return

The rate of return is calculated by taking the average of the cash-in flows and dividing by the original investment. Thus the following formula is required in cell B15.

AVERAGE(D4:D8)/C3

NPV at a fixed discount rate

The NPV function is used to calculate the net present value. This function requires reference to the discount rate and the cash-in flows. The following formula is required in cell B16:

NPV(B9,D4:D8)–C3

Note that it is necessary to subtract the original investment after the NPV function.

Profitability index (PI)

The PI also uses the NPV function, but the result is divided by the original investment as can be seen in the formula in cell B17:

NPV(B9,D4:D8)–C3

Internal rate of return

The IRR function is used to calculate the IRR in cell B18. This function requires reference to cash-in flows, but the first cell in the range must be the original investment expressed as a negative value. Furthermore the function requires a 'guess' to be entered as after the data range. Thus the formula for cell B28 is:

IRR(F3:F8,0.3)

NPV and PI at Variable Discount Rate

A separate work area is required to be able to calculate the NPV using a discount rate that varies from year to year. Figure 11.3 shows the work area required.

	A	B	C	D	E	F
49	Variable discount rate work area					
50	Year no.	1	2	3	4	5
51	Cash-Flow	60000	95000	120000	180000	200000
52	Discounted 1 period	48780	76613	96774	146341	163934
53	Discounted 2 periods	62287	61785	78044	118977	
54	Discounted 3 periods	50231	49826	62938		
55	Discounted 4 periods	40509	40182			
56	Discounted 5 periods	32669				
57						
58	Sum of Present Values	234477				
59	Net Present Value	-115523				
60	Profitability Index	0.67				

Figure 11.3 Variable discount rate work area

The NPV function assumes a constant rate of interest over the duration of the investment and therefore to accommodate an interest or discount rate that can change each year, the PV function needs to be used. In this context the PV function is used one year at a time and the discounted value is year by year picked up by a new PV function which adjusts it appropriately. In the example the cash-in flows have to be discounted over the five years.

In cells B51 to F51 the nominal cash flow amounts are discounted for one year using the following formula;

PV(B$11+$B$9,1,–B50)

Note that the PV function assumes that the cash flow value is negative (i.e. a credit) and in the above formula this has been reversed by the negative reference to B50. The reference to B11 has the row fixed with the $ which means that the formula can be copied holding the reference to row 11 absolute but changing the column reference. Figure 11.4 shows the formulae in the first two columns.

	A	B	C
48			
49	Variable discount rate		
50	Year no.	1	2
51	Cash-Flow	=D4	=D5
52	Discounted 1 period	=PV(B$11+$B$9,1,-B51)	=PV(C$11+$B$9,1,-C51)
53	Discounted 2 periods	=PV(B$11+B9,1,-C52)	=PV(C$11+$B$9,1,-C52)
54	Discounted 3 periods	=PV(B$11+$B$9,1,-C53)	=PV(C$11+$B$9,1,-C53)
55	Discounted 4 periods	=PV(B$11+$B$9,1,-C54)	=PV(C$11+$B$9,1,-C54)
56	Discounted 5 periods	=PV(B$11+$B$9,1,-C55)	
57			
58	Sum of Present Values	=SUM(B52:B56)	
59	Net Present Value	=B58-C3	
60	Profitability Index	=B58/C3	

Figure 11.4 Formulae for calculating NPV
at a variable discount rate

In rows 52 and 55 each future cash flow from year 2 to 5 is again discounted using a unique interest rate for each year until the cash flow in year 5 has been discounted 5 times and the cash flow in year has been discounted 4 times etc. The individual cash streams are then summed and in the usual way the investment is subtracted from this amount to produce the net present value.

LEARNING CURVE COSTING

The learning curve costing model is a deterministic plan that demonstrates how unit cost of production will vary as a result of improvements in the production process. The underlying assumption of this model is that the efficiency of labour and material utilisation will improve as the organisation learns from its experience in the manufacture of the product. Thus, unit costs will decrease as improvements in labour efficiency and material usage are effected. The model is on the CD accompanying this book under the name LEARN.

Developing the plan

The plan commences with a data input form in which all the key variables are specified. A first year production figure is required that can be held constant over time in order to see the effect of the improvements in material and labour. Alternatively the production figure can be increased in order to demonstrate the total effect of an increase in the scale of production, as well as improvements in efficiency.

The input data required for the plan are the first year's production, material costs per unit, labour cost per unit, fixed costs, annual growth production, learning curve effect for materials and labour and the price. The horizon for this plan has been set to 10 years.

The learning curve effect for materials is the percentage improvement in the use of materials that can be achieved per annum over the life of the project. This figure should also include improvement that the firm may achieve through a better buying policy, either due to eventual economies of scale, or from finding less expensive sources of the materials. The learning curve effect for labour includes increases in efficiency due to better skills, a higher degree of automation, as well as improved internal procedures. Figure 11.5 shows the plan with some sample data.

The sample data used in Figure 11.5 has no annual growth rate in production. The effect of this is to highlight the impact on the profit of the learning curve effect alone. If a growth rate in production is specified then the overall profit improvement would be even more dramatic. Therefore a formula is entered into cell C14 and copied for the remaining years, to accommodate a possible growth in production which is:

C13*(1+$B$7)

The formula for the variable costs in column E begins in year one by adding the material costs and labour costs and multiplying by the production. Thus the formula in cell E13 is:

($B$4+$B$5)*C13

	A	B	C	D	E	F	G	H	I
1	Learning Curve Costing over 10 Years								
2									
3	First year's production	2500							
4	Material costs per unit	35.25							
5	Labour costs per unit	25.50							
6	Fixed costs	75000							
7	Annual growth in production	0.00%							
8	Learning curve effect - Materials	5.00%							
9	Learning curve effect - Labour	15.00%							
10	Price	99.99							
11									
12			Year no.	Production	F.Costs	Var.Costs	Unit cost	Revenue		Profit Improvemer
13			1	2500	75000	151875	90.75	249975	23100	0
14			2	2500	75000	137906	85.16	249975	37069	6.56%
15			3	2500	75000	125592	80.24	249975	49383	6.14%
16			4	2500	75000	114707	75.88	249975	60268	5.74%
17			5	2500	75000	105056	72.02	249975	69919	5.36%
18			6	2500	75000	96476	68.59	249975	78499	5.00%
19			7	2500	75000	88823	65.53	249975	86152	4.67%
20			8	2500	75000	81978	62.79	249975	92997	4.36%
21			9	2500	75000	75835	60.33	249975	99140	4.07%
22			10	2500	75000	70306	58.12	249975	104669	3.80%

Figure 11.5 Learning curve costing model

In year two the learning curve effect for materials and labour is taken into consideration when calculating the variable costs, and therefore the formula in cell E14,which can be copied for the remaining years is:

($B$4*(1–$B$8)^B13+$B$5*(1-$B$9)^B13)*C14

The unit cost is calculated by adding the fixed and variable costs, and dividing by the production. Thus the formula in cell F13, which can be copied for the remaining years is:

(D13+E13)/C13

The revenue is the price multiplied by the production and therefore the formula in cell F13 which can be copied for the remaining years is:

C13*$B$10

The profit is the revenue less the production multiplied by the unit cost and therefore the formula in cell G13 which can be copied for the remaining years is:

G13–(F13*C13)

Finally the profit improvement percentage is calculated in column H. Clearly no improvement can be produced in year one and so a zero is entered into cell H13. In year two the improvement percentage is calculated by subtracting the profit in the previous year from the profit in the current year and dividing by the total costs. Therefore the formula required in cell H14 which can be copied for the remaining years is:

(H14–H13)/(D14+E14)

The cumulative affect of the learning curve can be seen not only by the percentage profit improvement, but also by the reduction in unit costs. The graph in Figure 11.6 illustrates this well.

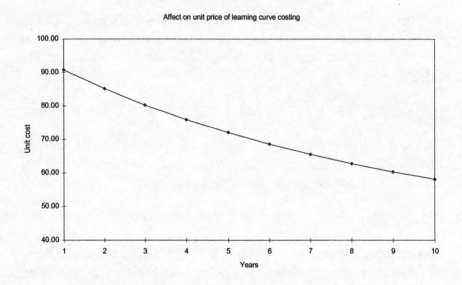

Figure 11.6 Learning curve costing chart

BREAK-EVEN ANALYSIS

The break-even analysis model is a deterministic plan that calculates the volume at which the firms' total costs are equal to the total revenue. The model is on the CD accompanying this book under the name **BREAKEVEN**. This level of volume is defined as the *break-even* point. The break-even point is derived by calculating the contribution per unit sold, which in turn is defined as the unit selling price less the unit variable cost. The unit contribution is then divided into the fixed costs and the result is the number of units that must be sold for the contribution to absorb the total fixed costs.

The break-even point is not a stationary concept. The volume required in order to pay the total cost continually changes over time due to changes in various costs and prices.

The plan shown here is designed to demonstrate the effect of inflation on the break-even point, which is achieved by providing a growth factor for the fixed costs, the variable costs and the price. When these figures have been entered the break-even point will automatically be extrapolated for four years.

The completed model is shown in Figure 11.7.

	A	B	C	D	E
1	Break-even analysis on Volume				
2					
3		YEAR 1	YEAR 2	YEAR 3	YEAR 4
4	Fixed Costs	6750	7425	8168	8984
5	Variable Costs	34.66	36.39	38.21	40.12
6	Selling Price	98.12	100.57	103.09	105.66
7					
8	Growth in Fixed Costs	10.00%			
9	Growth in Variable Costs	5.00%			
10	Growth in Selling Price	2.50%			
11					
12	Contribution	63.46	64.18	64.87	65.54
13					
14	Break-even unit production	106	116	126	137

Figure 11.7 Break-even point analysis

The formulae required to calculate the break-even point for the plan in Figure 11.7 are not complex and are shown in Figure 11.8.

	A	B	C	D	E
1	Break-even analysis on V				
2					
3		YEAR 1	YEAR 2	YEAR 3	YEAR 4
4	Fixed Costs	6750	=B4*(1+$B$8)	=C4*(1+$B$8)	=D4*(1+$B$8)
5	Variable Costs	34.66	=B5*(1+$B$9)	=C5*(1+$B$9)	=D5*(1+$B$9)
6	Selling Price	98.12	=B6*(1+$B$10)	=C6*(1+$B$10)	=D6*(1+$B$10)
7					
8	Growth in Fixed Costs	0.1			
9	Growth in Variable Costs	0.05			
10	Growth in Selling Price	0.025			
11					
12	Contribution	=B6-B5	=C6-C5	=D6-D5	=E6-E5
13					
14	Break-even unit production	=B4/B12	=C4/C12	=D4/D12	=E4/E12

Figure 11.8 Formulae for break-even analysis

The break-even analysis shown here assumes a single product situation and frequently this is not the case. Where multiple products are involved the fixed costs or overheads must first be apportioned and then a break-even point calculated for each product or product category. The result will be a break-even point statement for the firm as a whole, which will include a series of volumes, one for each product.

ECONOMIC ORDER QUANTITIES

There are a range of mathematical techniques available to assist with most aspects of production management, and particularly with the management and control of stock or inventory levels.

The economic order quantity model calculates the most efficient lot size in which inventory should be purchased. It is a production management technique that is used in many firms. The model is on the CD accompanying the book under the name EOQ.

This is an optimising model which is based on the assumption that the larger the order placed, the lower the costs of ordering will be. At the same time, the larger the order placed, the higher the carrying costs of stock will be. The economic order quantity model calculates an optimal level between these two conflicting cost curves.

The input required for the economic order quantity (EOQ) model are the annual usage in units (AUU), the unit price (UP), the variable cost per order (VCO) and the holding costs as a percentage (HC%). The formula for determining the EOQ is:

$$EOQ = \sqrt{(2 * AUU * VCO / UP * HC\%)}$$

In addition to indicating the lot size, this model is also used to evaluate a supplier's special offer to see whether or not it is worthwhile to purchase in volume in order to obtain a discount.

Developing the EOQ plan

The plan considers three scenarios. The first is the economic order quantity with no supplier discount policy, the second calculates the EOQ with a supplier discount policy and the third brings in some additional assumptions to calculate the EOQ with lead times and safety stock. Figure 11.9 shows the completed plan.

	A	B	C	D	E	F	G
1	ECONOMIC ORDER QUANTITY						
2		No Supplier policy	With Supplier policy		With lead times and safety stock		
3	Annual Usage in Units	1250	1250		Annual Usage in Units	1250	
4	Unit Price	60	48		Weekly Usage	24	
5	Variable Cost per Order	28	28		Unit Price	60	
6	Holding Cost as %	30%	30%		Variable Cost per Order	28	
7	Minimum Order		1250		Holding Cost as %	0	
8	EOQ	62	1250		Lead Time in Weeks	8	Assumption
9					Re-order Point	192	
10	Total Cost of Inventory				Possible Delivery Delay in Weeks	3	Assumption
11	Number of Orders	20	1		Possible Unforeseen Demand in %	3%	Assumption
12	Total Variable Costs	550	28		Safety Stock	74	
13	Average Inventory	31	625		EOQ	62	
14	Total Holding Costs	558	8906		Average Inventory	105	
15	Total Inventory Costs	1108	8934		No of Orders per year	21	
16					Cost of Safety & EOQ	30	
17	Cost of goods to Supplier	75000	59375		Cost of EOQ without Safety Stock	9	
18	Total Costs	76108	68309				
19							
20	Saving/cost of supplier policy	7799					

Figure 11.9 Economic Order Quantity

EOQ with no supplier policy

The required input for calculating the EOQ with no supplier policy is the annual usage in units, the unit price, the holding cost as a percentage and the variable cost per order. Using the equation for EOQ described above the formula required in cell B8 is:

ROUND(SQRT((2*B3*B5)/(B4*B6)),0)

The ROUND function has been incorporated in the above formula to ensure that the nearest whole number is returned as the EOQ.

EOQ with a supplier policy

One additional item of input is required for the calculation of the EOQ with a supplier policy and that is the minimum order requirement. For this example the unit price has been reduced from £60 to £47.50, but the supplier demands a minimum order of 1250 units. The formula required in cell C8 is therefore:

ROUND(MAX(SQRT((2*C3*C5)/(C4*C6)),C7),0)

The MAX function in the above formula compares the result of the SQRT part of the calculation with the minimum order and returns the larger number. Therefore if the annual usage is very large it will be more economical to purchase more than 1250 units.

Cost of inventory

It is important to know the cost of inventory both with and without the supplier discount policy in order that a comparison can be made to ascertain whether it is worth-while accepting the supplier discount. Figure 11.10 shows the formulae for this part of the plan.

As can be seen from Figure 11.10 although the cost of inventory is higher for the supplier policy scenario, the overall costs are still lower due to the lower selling price.

	A	B	C
10	**Total Cost of Inventory**		
11	Number of Orders	=ROUND(B3/B8,0)	=ROUND(C3/C8,0)
12	Total Variable Costs	=B11*B5	=C11*C5
13	Average Inventory	=ROUND(B8/2,0)	=ROUND(C8/2,0)
14	Total Holding Costs	=B13*B4*B6	=C13*C4*C6
15	Total Inventory Costs	=B14+B12	=C14+C12
16			
17	Cost of goods to Supplier	=B3*B4	=C3*C4
18	Total Costs	=B17+B15	=C17+C15
19			
20	Saving/cost of supplier policy	=B18-C18	

Figure 11.10 Formulae for calculating the cost of inventory

Lead times and safety stock

As it is likely that there will be a lead time between placing and receiving an order, this should be taken into consideration and a safety stock level be set which ensures that an order will be placed at the right time. The implications of this are calculated in the third part of this plan. Three further assumptions are made; the leadtime in weeks, the possible delivery delay in weeks and the possible percentage unforeseen demand. The calculations here have been done for no supplier policy, but could equally well include the supplier policy. Figure 11.11 shows the formulae required for this part of the plan.

SALES CAMPAIGN APPRAISAL

The sales campaign appraisal model is a deterministic plan that evaluates the cost of conducting a promotional sales campaign over a number of weeks. The plan reports on the likely number of prospects that will attend sales presentations and how many will be converted to sales. The model is on the CD accompanying the book under the name **CAMPAIGN**.

	E	F	G
1			
2	**With lead times and safety stock**		
3	Annual Usage in Units	=B3	
4	Weekly Usage	=F3/52	
5	Unit Price	=B4	
6	Variable Cost per Order	=B5	
7	Holding Cost as %	=B6	
8	Lead Time in Weeks	8	Assumption
9	Re-order Point	=F4*F8	
10	Possible Delivery Delay in Weeks	3	Assumption
11	Possible Unforeseen Demand in %	0.03	Assumption
12	Safety Stock	=(F4*F10)+(F4*F10*F11)	
13	**EOQ**	**=ROUND((SQRT((2*F3*F6)/(F5*F7)))+1,0)**	
14	Average Inventory	=F13/2+F12	
15	No of Orders per year	=ROUND((F3/F13)+1,0)	
16	Cost of Safety & EOQ	=(F13+F12/2)*F7	
17	Cost of EOQ without Safety Stock	=F13/2*F7	

Figure 11.11 Formulae for calculating lead times and safety stock

The sales campaign plan has been designed for 10 weeks of analysis after the initial promotion and requires the following input:

- initial promotion cost;
- duration of primary promotion in weeks;
- cost of a sales presentation;
- revenue per unit sold;
- cost per unit;
- conversion rate to sale at presentation as a percentage;
- estimate of the percentage of enquiries converted to sales presentation;
- estimate of the number of enquiries per week after promotion;
- erstimate of the number of prospects attending sales presentation who will eventually purchase.

Figure 11.12 shows the completed model with sample data.

	A	B	C	D	E	F	G	H	I	J	K	L
1	Sales Campaign Appraisal											
2												
3	Product				Widgets							
4	Initial promotion costs				155000							
5	Promotion duration in weeks				5							
6	Cost of sales presentation				775							
7	Conversion to sale at presentation %				40%							
8	Revenue per unit				3950							
9	Production cost per unit				1250							
10												
11	Weeks after promotion	No. of enquiries	Cum, enquiries	No. sales presentations	Cum. sales present's	Units sold	Cum. sales	Cost per presentation	Marketing cost per sale	Total cost	Total revenue	Profit on campaign
12	1	130	130	0	0	0	0	0				
13	2	190	320	47	47	18	18	4073	8611	213925	71100	-142825
14	3	250	570	67	114	26	44	1815	3523	261925	173800	-88125
15	4	440	1010	92	206	36	80	1099	1938	326300	316000	-10300
16	5	750	1760	142	348	56	136	762	1140	435050	537200	102150
17	6	555	2315	258	606	103	239	586	649	653700	944050	290350
18	7	300	2615	189	795	75	314	379	494	693975	1240300	546325
19	8	100	2715	93	888	37	351	256	442	665825	1386450	720625
20	9	25	2740	32	920	12	363	195	427	633550	1433850	800300
21	10	5	2745	8	928	3	366	174	423	618700	1445700	827000

Figure 11.12 Sales campaign appraisal model

Developing the sales campaign plan

The first step in the plan is to enter all the headings so that there is a structure for the model. Some sample data should be entered in order that the logic for the formulae can be checked as it is being developed.

The number of enquiries received each week after the initial promotion is an estimate. In this example it is assumed that the effects of the promotion increase over a five week period and then begin to drop off until there are only a few enquiries at the end of the 10 weeks.

The estimated numbers of sales presentations are assumed to be linked with the numbers of enquiries. In this example it is estimated to be between 30% and 40% of the previous week's enquiries. The values in the model are derived by a random number generator used in conjunction with a one period lag on the number of enquiries. The formula entered into cell D13, which is copied for the remaining weeks is:

In Excel:

```
INT(RAND()*0.1)+0.3)*B12
```

In 1-2-3:

INT(RAND*0.1)+0.3)*B12)

The RAND function in the above formula generates a random number between 0 and 1. However, by manipulating the result as shown in the above formula the result will always be between 30% and 40% of the previous week's number of enquiries.

The problem with the RAND function is that it is re-evaluated every time the spreadsheet is recalculated and therefore different values will be returned. Therefore having produced a series of estimated values these cells should be converted to values only. This is achieved by copying the range with the Edit Copy command and then selecting Paste Special Values. This removes the underlying formula leaving only the results in the cells.

The units sold are calculated by multiplying the number of sales presentations by the conversion to sale percentage. The following formula is required in cell F13, which can be copied for the remaining weeks:

INT(D13*$E$7)

The INT function has been incorporated into the formula to ensure that the result is rounded down to a whole number.

The cost per presentation is calculated by multiplying the cost per sales presentation by the number of presentations, adding that to the total cost of promotion and dividing by the cumulative sales presentation. The formula in cell H13 which is copied for the remaining weeks is:

($E$4+(D13*$E$6))/E13

The marketing cost per sale is the promotion cost divided by the cumulative sales, which means the following formula is required in cell I13:

$E$4/G13

The total costs are calculated as the promotion costs plus the cost of the sales presentations that week plus the production costs for units sold. The formula required in cell J13 is therefore:

$E$4+($E$6*D13)+(G13*$E$9)

The total revenue is the number of units sold multiplied by the revenue per unit and the profit on the campaign is therefore calculated as the total costs less the total revenue.

SUMMARY

In this chapter a number of different business plans have been developed in order to demonstrate some of the applications for which a spreadsheet can be used. It is hoped that readers will find some of the models directly applicable but the techniques shown can also be applied in a number of complimentary areas.

What-if Analysis

Good judgment is usually the result of experience. And experience is frequently the result of bad judgment.

R. E. Neustadt and E. R. May, *Thinking in Time*, New York: The Free Press, 1986.

INTRODUCTION

What-if analysis may be defined as the technique of asking specific questions about the result of a change or of a series of changes to assumptions in a model or a business plan.

What-if analysis has been performed manually for decades before the arrival of computers. In the spreadsheet environment, however, it is a direct product of the fact that once a model or plan has been entered into the computer, it may be recalculated again and again. It allows the user to change assumptions concerning input data or input relationships, and to recalculate a model to see the impact of these changes on critical output values.

Typical what-if questions might be to ask what effect will a 2% increase in direct labour costs have on profit and return on investment? What effect will a further 30 day delay in receiving cash from the debtors have on the overdraft and/or return on investment?

What-if questions may be considered one at a time, or several at once. If it is necessary to investigate the effect of two simultaneous changes in the assumptions, then it is usually advantageous to also consider these changes in isolation, i.e. one at a time, so that their individual effects, as well as their joint effects, will be known. Irrespective of whether single or multiple changes to input are made, several factors or objectives will usually be monitored.

In addition to what-if analysis there are two other related concepts which should also be considered. These concepts are *goal seeking* or *backward iteration* and *sensitivity analysis*.

Goal seeking is a technique whereby a model calculates the value of an input variable that is required in order to achieve a stated output objective. For example, using goal seeking the system could calculate the level of sales required for a return on investment of 25%. Thus the goal seeking procedure requires an input variable, which is usually considered the models' output, and the result is the value for a variable that is normally input to the model. Spreadsheets typically have a built-in command for this, which will be discussed later in this chapter.

Sensitivity analysis is a technique that ascertains the relative importance of specified input variables in a business scenario or plan. This is achieved by calculating the result of a number of relatively small changes in the specified input factors on the objective function, or output of the business model. These input and output changes are then compared to ascertain which variables have the greatest impact. The user of sensitivity analysis is concerned to establish whether a 5% increase in raw material costs, or a 2% increase in labour costs will have the worse impact on the profit of the business.

Sensitivity analysis and what-if analysis are quite different, although the terms are often used interchangeably.

THREE APPROACHES TO WHAT-IF ANALYSIS

With spreadsheet models there are several possible levels of what-if and associated analysis available, which can be described in terms of the following three categories:

1. what-if analysis on opening assumptions;
2. what-if tables;
3. backward iteration or goal seeking.

Each of these will be considered separately in this chapter.

WHAT-IF ANALYSIS ON OPENING ASSUMPTIONS

What-if analysis on opening values is the simplest case and is performed by placing the cursor on the appropriate input cell and entering a new assumption. Because spreadsheets are developed using cell references, all cells which refer directly, or indirectly, to the cell being changed will be recalculated based on the revised input. Providing recalculation is set to automatic, the spreadsheet is immediately recalculated and the effect of the new assumption can be seen. This approach to the what-if technique is especially suitable when first period data assumptions such as price, opening sales volumes etc. are to be changed.

Figure 12.1 shows the 12 month business plan that will be used throughout this chapter and Figure 12.2 shows the effect that reducing the opening sales volume has on the net profit. This plan can be found on the CD accompanying the book under the name **BUSPLAN.**

Providing any growth or cost factors have been separated from the model any input assumption can be changed using this technique. Furthermore if a data input form has been created as was shown in Chapter 9 it is easier to see the input data that can be changed.

	A	B	C	D	E	F	G	H	I	J	K	L	M	N
1	Business Plan													
2														
3		JAN	FEB	MAR	APR	MAY	JUN	JUL	AUG	SEP	OCT	NOV	DEC	TOTAL
4	Income													
5	Volume	9750	9849	9948	10049	10151	10254	10358	10462	10568	10675	10783	10893	123740
6	Unit Price	50	50	50	50	50	50	50	50	50	50	50	50	50
7	Turnover	482625	487512	492248	497434	502470	507558	512697	517888	523131	528428	533778	539183	6125151
8														
9	Expenditure													
10	Raw Materia	190125	192050	193995	195959	197943	199947	201971	204016	206082	208169	210276	212405	2412938
11	Direct Labou	112750	112750	112750	112750	112750	112750	112750	112750	112750	112750	112750	112750	1353000
12	Energy Con	34125	34471	34820	35172	35528	35888	36251	36618	36989	37364	37742	38124	433091
13	Total Direct	337000	339271	341564	343881	346221	348585	350973	353385	355821	358282	360768	363279	4199030
14	Gross Profi	145625	148241	150884	153553	156249	158973	161724	164503	167310	170146	173010	175903	1926121
15														
16	Other Costs													
17	Administrati	14625	14773	14923	15074	15226	15381	15536	15694	15852	16013	16175	16339	185611
18	Commission	2413	2438	2462	2487	2512	2538	2563	2589	2616	2642	2669	2696	30626
19	Depreciation	19500	19697	19897	20098	20302	20507	20715	20925	21137	21351	21567	21785	247481
20	Interest	1200	1200	1200	1200	1200	1200	1200	1200	1200	1200	1200	1200	14400
21	Maintenance	3370	3393	3416	3439	3462	3486	3510	3534	3558	3583	3608	3633	41990
22	Salaries	75000	75000	75000	75000	75000	75000	75000	75000	75000	75000	75000	75000	900000
23	Travel	4550	4550	4550	4550	4550	4550	4550	4550	4550	4550	4550	4550	54600
24	Total Other	120658	121051	121447	121848	122253	122662	123074	123492	123913	124339	124768	125203	1474708
25														
26	Net Profit B	24967	27190	29436	31705	33996	36311	38650	41011	43397	45807	48242	50701	451414

Figure 12.1 Business plan before performing what-if analysis

	A	B	C	D	E	F	G	H	I	J	K	L	M	N
1	**Business Plan**	JAN	FEB	MAR	APR	MAY	JUN	JUL	AUG	SEP	OCT	NOV	DEC	TOTAL
2														
3														
4	*Income*													
5	Volume	8000	8081	8163	8245	8329	8413	8498	8585	8671	8759	8848	8938	101531
6	Unit Price	50	50	50	50	50	50	50	50	50	50	50	50	50
7	**Turnover**	**396000**	**400010**	**404060**	**408151**	**412283**	**416458**	**420674**	**424934**	**429236**	**433582**	**437972**	**442407**	**5025765**
8														
9	*Expenditure*													
10	Raw Materia	156000	157580	159175	160787	162415	164059	165720	167398	169093	170805	172534	174281	1979847
11	Direct Labou	112750	112750	112750	112750	112750	112750	112750	112750	112750	112750	112750	112750	1353000
12	Energy Con	28000	28284	28570	28859	29151	29446	29745	30046	30350	30657	30968	31281	355357
13	Total Direct	296750	298613	300495	302396	304316	306256	308215	310194	312193	314212	316252	318313	3688204
14	**Gross Profi**	**99250**	**101397**	**103565**	**105755**	**107967**	**110202**	**112459**	**114740**	**117043**	**119370**	**121720**	**124094**	**1337561**
15														
16	*Other Costs*													
17	Administrati	12000	12122	12244	12368	12493	12620	12748	12877	13007	13139	13272	13406	152296
18	Commissior	1980	2000	2020	2041	2061	2082	2103	2125	2146	2168	2190	2212	25129
19	Depreciatior	16000	16162	16326	16491	16658	16827	16997	17169	17343	17518	17696	17875	203061
20	Interest	1200	1200	1200	1200	1200	1200	1200	1200	1200	1200	1200	1200	14400
21	Maintenanc	2968	2986	3005	3024	3043	3063	3082	3102	3122	3142	3163	3183	36882
22	Salaries	75000	75000	75000	75000	75000	75000	75000	75000	75000	75000	75000	75000	900000
23	Travel	4550	4550	4550	4550	4550	4550	4550	4550	4550	4550	4550	4550	54600
24	Total Other	113698	114020	114345	114674	115006	115341	115680	116022	116368	116717	117070	117426	1386368
25														
26	**Net Profit B**	**-14448**	**-12623**	**-10780**	**-8919**	**-7039**	**-5139**	**-3221**	**-1283**	**675**	**2652**	**4650**	**6667**	**-48807**

Figure 12.2 Business plan after reduced opening volume

Occasionally it might be necessary to see the effect of changing the actual logic of a plan. Extreme care must be taken in this case because changing the logic of plans that have been tried and tested can have knock-on effects that might not be obvious to the individual making the changes.

WHAT-IF TABLES

Spreadsheets provide a powerful what-if facility referred to as *what-if* or *data* tables. Data tables allow a range of what-if questions to be calculated at one time, by setting up a table in which a range of possible input values are specified together with a reference to required output. For example, a data table can be established to report the effect of changing the sales volume growth rate on the gross profit, net profit, return on investment and cash in bank for all integer growth rates of sales volume between 0.5% and 10%.

There are two main types of data table, which are the 1-way table, and the 2-way table. A 1-way table allows a single input factor to be analysed against as many output variables as the user requires. The input factor is a cell in the plan that is to change and the output factors are those cells on which you want to see the effect of the change. For example in the business plan the input factor might be the opening volume and the output factors might be the gross profit and net profit figures for July and December.

In the case of a 2-way table two input factors, and a single output variable can be specified. In the business plan for example, the input factors might be the opening sales volume and the opening price and the output factor might be the year end net profit.

Some spreadsheets, including 1-2-3, allow for a 3-way table through the use of multiple spreadsheets. In this situation – taking the business plan – it would be possible to construct a table that looked at changes to the opening sales volume, the opening unit price and the cost of raw materials and reported the combined effect on the year end net profit.

Before the Data Table command in Excel or the Range What-if command in 1-2-3 can be used the spreadsheet needs to be prepared with the necessary information for the command to calculate.

Creating a 1-way data table

In the case of a 1-way table, a range of input values must first be entered into a suitable area of the spreadsheet, and references to the formulae on which the analysis is to be performed must be made.

Figure 12.3 shows the outline of a table to analyse varying volume rates against the gross profit and net profit before tax for December in the business plan.

	A	B	C	D	E
29	Data Table to see the effect of changing sales volume				
30	on gross and net profit for December				
31					
32		G. Profit	N. Profit		
33		175903	50701		
34	8000				
35	8250				
36	8500				
37	8750				
38	9000				
39	9250				
40	9500				
41	9750				
42	10000				
43	10250				
44	10500				
45					

Figure 12.3 Outline of a 1-way data table

The values in the range A34 through A44 can be entered either by typing in the values, using a Fill technique or they maybe the result of a formula. In this example the values are in ascending order at regular intervals, but this is not necessary for the command to work. Cells B33 and C33 contain references to cells M12 and M22 in the business plan, which are the gross profit and net profit figures for December.

The exact form of the command for evaluating the table will vary between different spreadsheets, but in all cases it is necessary to first highlight the range into which the table information has been entered, which in the above example is A33 through C44. The command for accessing the table dialogue box in Excel is Data Table, and in 1-2-3 is Range Analyse What-if. Figures 12.4 and 12.5 show these two dialogue boxes.

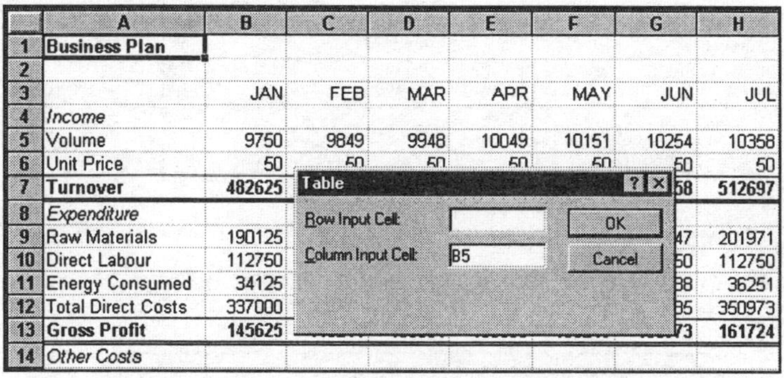

Figure 12.4 Excel data table dialogue box

In the case of 1-2-3 the number of input variables is specified which in Figure 12.5 is 1 because this is a 1-way table. The cell in the model representing this input variable is then specified, which is the sales volume in cell B5.

In Excel the input data as shown in Figure 12.3 can be in a column or a row. In this example it is in a column and thus the reference to the sales volume in cell B5 of the model is entered into the column input cell.

	A	B	What-if Table					G
1	Business Plan 1		Number of variables: 1		OK			
2		1					5	6
3		JAN	Table range:		Cancel		AY	JUN
4	Income		B49..H58					
5	Volume	9750			Reset		51	10254
6	Unit Price	50	Input cell 1:				50	50
7	Turnover	482625	B5				70	507558
8			Input cell 2:					
9	Expenditure							
10	Raw Materials	190125					43	199947
11	Direct Labour	112750	Input cell 3:				50	112750
12	Energy Consumed	34125					28	35888
13	Total Direct Costs	337000					21	348585
14			Formula cell:					
15	Gross Profit	145625					49	158973
16								
17	Administration	14625	14773	14923	15074	15226		15381
18	Commission	2413	2438	2462	2487	2512		2538
19	Depreciation	19500	19697	19897	20098	20302		20507
20	Interest	1200	1200	1200	1200	1200		1200

Figure 12.5 1-2-3 What-if table dialogue box

On clicking OK after completing the dialogue box the table is completed and will be displayed as shown in Figure 12.6.

	A	B	C	D	E
29	Data Table to see the effect of changing sales volume				
30	on gross and net profit for December				
31					
32		G. Profit	N. Profit		
33		175903	50701		
34	8000	124093.9	6667.459		
35	8250	131495.3	12957.93		
36	8500	138896.6	19248.39		
37	8750	146298	25538.86		
38	9000	153699.4	31829.33		
39	9250	161100.7	38119.8		
40	9500	168502.1	44410.26		
41	9750	175903.5	50700.73		
42	10000	183304.9	56991.2		
43	10250	190706.2	63281.67		
44	10500	198107.6	69572.13		
45					

Figure 12.6 Results of a 1-way data table

The results produced by the table equate to having entered 8000 into cell B5 and then recording the gross profit and net profit figures for December, then 8250 is entered into cell B5 and the gross profit and net profit figures for December again recorded. This reiterative process would continue until all the required values for sales volume had been entered and the profit results recorded. The Data Table or What-if command performs this reiteration extremely quickly.

It is important to always have a way of cross-checking the results of any spreadsheet report in an attempt to validate the figures. The table in Figure 12.6 can be checked by looking at row 41 which gives the values when the opening volume is 9750 – as it is in the main plan – and these values should correspond to the values at the top of the table in cells B33 and C33.

Creating a 2-way table

A 2-way table requires input data is for two variables. For example, to analyse varying sales volume figures and unit prices on the net profit before tax in December in the business plan, the table specifications in Figure 12.7 are required.

	A	B	C	D	E	F	G	H
51	Data Table to see the effect of changing sales volume							
52	and unit price on the net profit for December							
53								
54					**Unit Price**			
55		50701	35	40	45	50	55	60
56		8000						
57		8250						
58		8500						
59	V	8750						
60	o	9000						
61	l	9250						
62	u	9500						
63	m	9750						
64	e	10000						
65		10250						
66		10500						
67								

Figure 12.7 Input data for a 2–way data table

The table area is selected in the same way as for the 1-way table, but when the dialogue box is accessed it is necessary this time to specify the first or column input cell as the sales volume in cell B5, and the second or row input cell as the unit price in cell B6. The results of this table are shown in Figure 12.8.

The results of this table are interesting, as it is clear that if the unit price is reduced to £45, a minimum of 9750 units must be produced to be in profit by the end of the year. But, if the price can be held at 50, the opening sales volume can be as little at 8000 and still leave a net profit at the end of the year.

In validating the accuracy of this table by taking a sales volume figure of 9750 and a price of 50, which is the data in the main model, the resulting net profit in the table should be the same as the net profit in the model (which is shown in cell A51 of the table). Looking at the table this is not the case as the net profit is showing 56120 as opposed to the 50701 that would be expected. Close examination of the main plan will show that the unit price is actually 49.5, but the row has been formatted to a whole number and it therefore displaying 50. If the opening price in the model is changed to 50 the net profit for December in the model will be 56120 as it is in the table.

	A	B	C	D	E	F	G	H
51	Data Table to see the effect of changing sales volume							
52	and unit price on the net profit for December							
53								
54					Unit Price			
55		50701	35	40	45	50	55	60
56		8000	115576	159891	204205	248520	292835	337150
57		8250	125302	171007	216711	262415	308120	353824
58		8500	135029	182123	229217	276310	323404	370498
59	V	8750	144755	193239	241722	290205	338689	387172
60	o	9000	154482	204355	254228	304100	353973	403846
61	l	9250	164209	215471	266733	317995	369258	420520
62	u	9500	173935	226587	279239	331890	384542	437194
63	m	9750	183662	237703	291744	345785	399827	453868
64	e	10000	193388	248819	304250	359680	415111	470542
65		10250	203115	259935	316755	373576	430396	487216
66		10500	212841	271051	329261	387471	445680	503890
67								

Figure 12.7 Completed 2-way data table

Excel data tables and 1-2-3 what-if tables

There are some important differences in the way Excel and 1-2-3 calculate data tables. In Excel the command actually places a formula using the TABLE function into each of the cells in the table range. Therefore if any changes are made to data in the main plan, or to the input or output ranges the table will automatically be recalculated to reflect the changes. This also means that there can be multiple data tables on a spreadsheet and all can be kept up-to-date simultaneously. In fact sometimes when working with very large tables, or many tables, the recalculation time can become unacceptable and therefore there is an option in Tools Options Calculations to set recalculation to Automatic except Tables which means that it will be necessary to press F9 to recalculate the data tables.

In 1-2-3 the command leaves absolute values as the results in the cells and thus if changes are made to the main plan or to the input or output data it is necessary to re-evaluate the table. If there is only one what-if table on the spreadsheet this can quickly be achieved by pressing the F8 Table function key. However this will only recalculate the *active* table, or the last one to be evaluated. Therefore if there are multiple tables on a spreadsheet they must be individually re-evaluated when changes are made.

A disadvantage of data tables in Excel is the fact that they must be located on the same worksheet as the input data, which effectively means that it is not possible to have a separate worksheet on which all the data tables for an application are placed. This is not a problem in 1-2-3 as tables can be located on separate sheets.

Creating a 3-way table in 1-2-3

1-2-3 has the facility to produce a 3-way what-if table. For example, to analyse the combined affect of changes in opening sales volume, unit price and the cost of raw materials a 3-way table can be used.

The first step in setting up this table is to prepare a table outline with the sales volume and unit price variables as for the 2-way table. For clarity the first part of the table has been placed on a new worksheet. The next step is to insert as many worksheets as there are values to be used as input for the third variable, which in this example is cost of raw materials. The two-dimensional outline is then copied to the same position on the other sheets. The data for the third variable is then entered into the top left corner of each sheet.

Figure 12.8 shows three of the sheets after selecting View Split Perspective.

The Range Analyse What-if command can now be issued and the boxes completed for a 3-way table. Because the top left corner of the table is used for the third variable, the output cell reference is located elsewhere, and in this example the reference to December's net profit in cell M22 of the main plan has been placed on sheet B, cell A12. Figure 12.9 shows the completed dialogue box for the 3-way table and Figure12.10 shows the results.

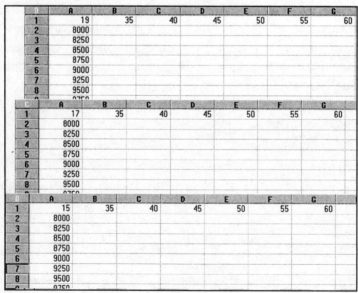

	A	B	C	D	E	F	G
1	19	35	40	45	50	55	60
2	8000						
3	8250						
4	8500						
5	8750						
6	9000						
7	9250						
8	9500						

	A	B	C	D	E	F	G
1	17	35	40	45	50	55	60
2	8000						
3	8250						
4	8500						
5	8750						
6	9000						
7	9250						
8	9500						

	A	B	C	D	E	F	G
1	15	35	40	45	50	55	60
2	8000						
3	8250						
4	8500						
5	8750						
6	9000						
7	9250						
8	9500						

Figure 12.8 Perspective view of multiple sheets in 1-2-3

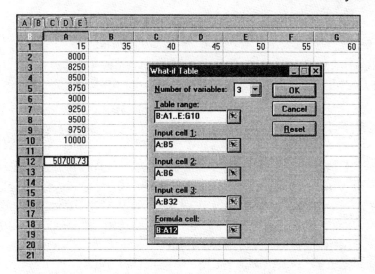

Figure 12.9 Dialogue box for 3-way table in 1-2-3

	A	B	C	D	E	F	G
1	19	35	40	45	50	55	60
2	8000	-117765	-73300.9	-28836.8	15627.31	60091.4	104555.5
3	8250	-115363	-69509.4	-23655.8	22197.77	68051.36	113905
4	8500	-112961	-65718	-18474.9	28768.23	76011.33	123254.4
5	8750	-110559	-61926.5	-13293.9	35338.7	83971.29	132603.9
6	9000	-108157	-58135	-8112.94	41909.16	91931.26	141953.4
7	9250	-105755	-54343.6	-2931.98	48479.62	99891.22	151302.8
8	9500	-103353	-50552.1	2248.98	55050.08	107851.2	160652.3

	A	B	C	D	E	F	G
1	17	35	40	45	50	55	60
2	8000	-99711.2	-55247.1	-10783	33681.07	78145.16	122609.2
3	8250	-96745.1	-50891.5	-5037.88	40815.71	86669.3	132522.9
4	8500	-93778.9	-46535.8	707.2607	47950.35	95193.45	142436.5
5	8750	-90812.8	-42180.2	6452.401	55085	103717.6	152350.2
6	9000	-87846.7	-37824.6	12197.54	62219.64	112241.7	162263.8
7	9250	-84880.5	-33468.9	17942.68	69354.28	120765.9	172177.5
8	9500	-81914.4	-29113.3	23687.82	76488.93	129290	182091.1

	A	B	C	D	E	F	G
1	15	35	40	45	50	55	60
2	8000	-81657.4	-37193.3	7270.741	51734.83	96198.92	140663
3	8250	-78127.1	-32273.5	13580.06	59433.65	105287.2	151140.8
4	8500	-74596.8	-27353.7	19889.38	67132.47	114375.6	161618.7
5	8750	-71066.5	-22433.9	26198.7	74831.3	123463.9	172096.5
6	9000	-67536.2	-17514.1	32508.02	82530.12	132552.2	182574.3
7	9250	-64005.9	-12594.3	38817.34	90228.94	141640.5	193052.1
8	9500	-60475.5	-7674.44	45126.66	97927.77	150728.9	203530

Figure 12.10 Completed 3-way table in 1-2-3

Looking at the results in the above table it can be seen that with a cost of raw materials of £15 per unit and a selling price of £45, an opening sales volume of 8000 is sufficient to return a net profit by December. However, if the cost of raw materials rises to £19 per unit it will be necessary to have an opening sales volume of 9500 in order to hold the price at £45 and return a net profit in December.

BACKWARD ITERATION OR GOAL SEEKING

Having developed a spreadsheet model for the purposes of profit planning, the results calculated are not always entirely satisfactory to the decision makers. A typical example might be when the profit plan shows a projected 10% return on investment (ROI), but the management require a 15% ROI. In these circumstances what-if analysis can be performed on the basic assumptions in the model, in order to determine what values of sales for example would be required to achieve the desired ROI for the business.

This procedure can, however, be a lengthy one because a large number of changes to the assumptions may have to be made before the model produces the required results. It was to provide a quick method of finding appropriate input values for a required result or outcome that backward iteration or goal seeking techniques have been included in spreadsheet packages.

Using the goal seeking feature

In the business plan the net profit in December is £50,701. The Goal Seek feature in Excel or Backsolver in 1-2-3 can be used to see what the opening sales volume would have to be in order for the December net profit to be £60,000 (taking all the other assumptions made in the model into consideration).

Goal Seek is accessed by selecting Tools Goal Seek and the dialogue box shown in Figure 12.11 is displayed and has to be filled out with the appropriate information.

	B	C	D	E	F	G	H	I	J
4									
5	9750	9849	9948	10049	10151	10254	10358	10462	10568
6	50	50	50	50	50	50	50	50	50
7	482625	487512	492448	497434	502470	507558	512697	517888	523131
8									
9									
10	190125	192050	19399	Goal Seek				? X	206082
11	112750	112750	11275	Set cell: $M$26		OK			112750
12	34125	34471	3482	To value: 60000					36989
13	337000	339271	34156			Cancel			355821
14	145625	148241	15088	By changing cell: B5					167310
15									
16									
17	14625	14773	14923	15074	15226	15381	15536	15694	15852

Figure 12.11 Excel Goal Seek dialogue box

In 1-2-3 a similar dialogue box is accessed by selecting Range Analyse Backsolver and this is shown in Figure 12.12. The only difference between 1-2-3 and Excel is that a contiguous range of cells in 1-2-3 can be changed, whereas in Excel it is restricted to a single cell.

	A	B	C	D	E	F	G	H	I
2		1	2	3	4	5	6	7	8
3		JAN	FEB	MAR	APR	MAY	JUN	JUL	AUG
4	*Income*								
5	Volume	9750	9849	9948	10049	10151	10254	10358	10462
6	Unit Price	50	Backsolver				X	50	50
7	Turnover	482625	Make cell:	A:M26		OK	8	512697	517888
8									
9	*Expenditure*		Equal to value:	60000		Cancel			
10	Raw Materials	190125					47	201971	204016
11	Direct Labour	112750	By changing cell(s): A:B5				50	112750	112750
12	Energy Consumed	34125					88	36251	36618
13	Total Direct Costs	337000	339271	341564	343881	346221	348585	350973	353385
14	Gross Profit	145625	148241	150884	153553	156249	158973	161724	164503
15									

Figure 12.12 1-2-3 Backsolver dialogue box

On clicking OK the spreadsheet is recalculated and the opening volume required in order to attain a year end net profit of £60,000 is displayed in cell B5. In this case the answer is 10,120.

Use Solver for optimising

Although Goal Seek and Backsolver are useful tools, they are restrictive because as can be seen from the previous example it was only possible to set a specific cell to a specified value by changing a single cell. It is often necessary to set parameters within which changes can be made and to be able to change ranges of cells as opposed to only a single cell.

To cope with this situation the spreadsheets have another feature called Solver. With Solver a number of different cells in different parts of the spreadsheet can be changed and constraints can be specified to ensure certain parameters are met, such as units produced in a production model cannot exceed a given number, or advertising expenditure cannot be a negative value. The output cell can be a specified value or it can be the maximum possible solution or the minimum possible solution, so that, for example, the maximum profit for varying units of production can be found or the minimum profit within the same constraints could be returned.

Solver requires the model to be set up with the required data and constraints before the analysis can be performed. Figure 12.13 shows a salesman's productivity model that will be used in this example. This file can be found on the CD accompanying this book under the name SALESMAN. The aim is to find the maximum profit that can be made by the sales team. Note that the constraints in Figure 12.13 are at this stage only text entries for information purposes.

	A	B	C	D
1	SALESMAN'S PRODUCTIVITY MODEL			
2				
3		NO. OF	PROFIT	TOTAL
4	SALESMAN	SALES	PER SALE	PROFIT
5	Higgins	40	30	1200
6	Dolittle	40	45	1800
7	Spock	40	25	1000
8	Jekyll	30	36	1080
9	TOTAL	150		5080
10				
11				
12	CONSTRAINTS			
13	Higgins	Minimum quota is 20 sales		
14	Dolittle	Minimum quota is 10 sales		
15	Spock	Minimum quota is 30 sales		
16	Jekyll	Minimum quota is 25 sales		
17	Total	Total number of sales must be 150		

Figure 12.13 Salesman's productivity model before optimising

Each sales person has a minimum quota that he or she is required to attain and the firm is dependent on a total sales figure of 150 units. Each sales person is responsible for a different product and the profit per sale, which is different for each product, has been entered into the model in column C. The adjustable cells are B5 through B8 which represent the number of sales per person.

Some values must be entered into these cells before using Solver, but they will be replaced during the analysis.

Having set up the spreadsheet Tools Solver in Excel or Range Analyse Solver in 1-2-3 is selected and the Solver Parameters dialogue box is displayed as shown in Figure 12.14 for Excel and Figure 12.15 for 1-2-3.

In Excel, as can be seen in Figure 12.14, the *target* cell is the total sales in cell D9 and the intention is to *maximise* this value by *changing* cells B5 through B8. These changes are *subject to the constraints* that have been specified on the spreadsheet in Figure 12.12.

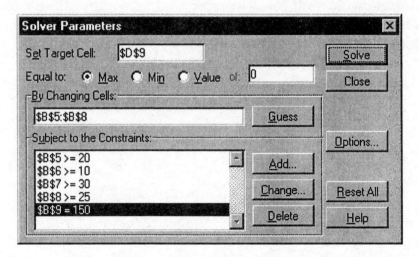

Figure 12.14 Excel Solver dialogue box

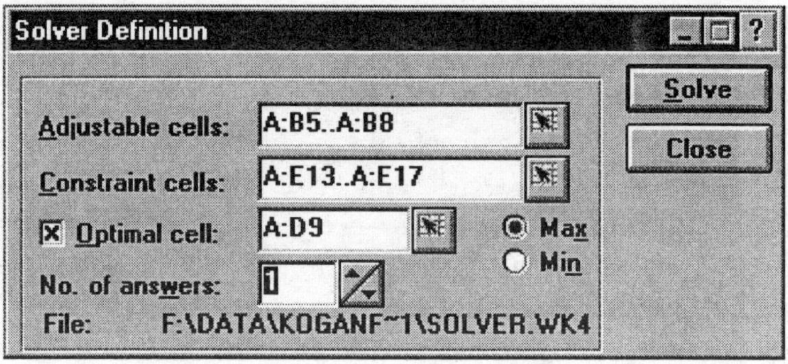

Figure 12.15 1-2-3 Solver dialogue box

In 1-2-3, as can be seen in Figure 12.15, the *adjustable* cells are those which can be changed by Solver; but the changes are subject to the criteria entered into the *Constraint cells*. In 1-2-3 it is necessary to enter the conditions for the constraints into the spreadsheet, as opposed to the Solver dialogue box which is the case with Excel. Figure 12.16 shows these entries which have been formatted to text. If the cells are not formatted to text they will display 0 as, at this stage, the conditions are all false. If a condition is true a 1 will be displayed. However, it is more useful in this situation to see the condition that Solver is using.

	A	B	C	D	E
1	SALESMAN'S PRODUCTIVITY MODEL				
2					
3		NO. OF	PROFIT	TOTAL	
4	SALESMAN	SALES	PER SALE	PROFIT	
5	Higgins	40	30	1200	
6	Dolittle	40	45	1800	
7	Spock	40	25	1000	
8	Jekyll	30	36	1080	
9	TOTAL	150		5080	
10					
11					
12	CONSTRAINTS				
13	Higgins	Minimum quota is 20 sales			+B5>=20
14	Dolittle	Minimum quota is 10 sales			+B6>=10
15	Spock	Minimum quota is 30 sales			+B7>=30
16	Jekyll	Minimum quota is 25 sales			+B8>=25
17	Total	Total number of sales must be 150			+B9=150
18					

Figure 12.16 Conditions entered into 1-2-3 spreadsheet

By checking the *Optimal cell* box in the Solver dialogue box 1-2-3 Solver will seek the optimal answer and in this case that is to be the *Max* value for cell D9. Only 1 answer is required for this example. By changing the use of the optimal box and the number of answers it is possible to have Solver produce multiple solutions that comply with the constraints specified.

Figure 12.17 shows the spreadsheet after *Solve* is selected from the dialogue box. The results are the same for both 1-2-3 and Excel.

It is possible to specify a problem that has no solution which means that there is no set of adjustable cell values that will satisfy all of the constraints made. For example, if an additional constraint of total profit to be greater than 10000 is added to the above example, Solver attempts to find a solution and then reports that no feasible answer could be found.

	A	B	C	D
1	SALESMAN'S PRODUCTIVITY MODEL			
2				
3		NO. OF	PROFIT	TOTAL
4	SALESMAN	SALES	PER SALE	PROFIT
5	Higgins	20	30	600
6	Dolittle	75	45	3375
7	Spock	30	25	750
8	Jekyll	25	36	900
9	TOTAL	150		5625
10				
11				
12	CONSTRAINTS			
13	Higgins	Minimum quota is 20 sales		
14	Dolittle	Minimum quota is 10 sales		
15	Spock	Minimum quota is 30 sales		
16	Jekyll	Minimum quota is 25 sales		
17	Total	Total number of sales must be 150		

Figure 12.17 Spreadsheet after using Solver

The example used here to illustrate Solver is a simple one and serves merely as an introduction to a feature that can perform very sophisticated analysis. Possible applications include solving simultaneous linear and non-linear equations, optimising investment yield, production level planning, staff scheduling models and many more.

SUMMARY

The ability of a spreadsheet to perform what-if analysis provides the necessary flexibility that enables financial managers and accountants to become power users. The speed of recalculation and the ease of change make this perhaps the single most important reason for the success of spreadsheet technology. It is important to remember however that the success of any kind of what-if or sensitivity analysis is entirely dependent on the correct development of the basic plan and the ability to interpret what the results might mean.

The goal seeking and solver features that are now available in most spreadsheets allow for powerful optimising techniques to be applied to a range of business plans.

Risk Analysis

*There is an intrinsic impermanence in industry and indeed the
management task is to recreate the company in a new form every year.*

Sir John Harvey-Jones, *Making it Happen – Reflections on Leadership*,
Fontana Collins, 1988.

INTRODUCTION

Most business plans or models are deterministic which means that
they rely on the use of a single point estimate for input data and
assumptions. Under conditions of uncertainty, which is the most
common environment in which business plans are developed, it is
frequently not possible to produce accurate estimates using a single
point approach and thus it is generally thought to be more
reasonable and realistic to specify input data as ranges.

For example, to say that the sales volume for the next period
will be between 8500 and 12,500 will offer a greater probability of
being right than a single point estimate of, say, 10,000. Similarly,
to specify the average sales price as being between 45 and 52, will
often have a greater chance of being correct than a single projection
of 50.

The structure of a deterministic plan, by its very nature, cannot
cope with input data specified as ranges. However, it is possible to
develop a model which enhances a deterministic, single point

estimate plan to allow data in the form of ranges to be incorporated, and which in effect converts the plan from a deterministic to a *probabilistic or stochastic* or *risk analysis* model. Risk analysis is also sometimes called probabilistic modelling, stochastic modelling, or Monte Carlo modelling.

Having specified input data as ranges the spreadsheet needs to recalculate the model thousands of times using numbers randomly chosen between the minimum and maximum values stated in the range. After each calculation the spreadsheet stores the required result. For example, to see the effect of a range of input data for the investment amount in the Capital Investment Appraisal model on the NPV at a fixed interest rate, it would be necessary to recalculate the model using different investment amounts and to collect the NPV result for each calculation. After a considerable number of recalculations, preferably thousands, a frequency distribution of the results is created and a graph drawn. This graph will, in general, be a bell shaped curve and the precise shape of the curve will reflect the degree of risk that is present in the investment based on the input data ranges.

PREPARING A PLAN FOR RISK ANALYSIS

It is usual to begin risk analysis from a fully tested deterministic plan or model. This is because it is difficult to develop a plan and be able to test the results of the underlying logic when ranges of data are used.

However, by carefully designing the original plan it is not difficult to adapt it for risk analysis and the example in this chapter uses the Capital Investment Appraisal plan developed in Chapter 10.

The completed risk analysis model will use four separate worksheets. The first sheet, called *CIA Model*, is the original Capital Investment Appraisal plan. The amended data from the original plan is on a shcet called *Risk Model*, the input form worksheet is called *Input*, the risk analysis results worksheet is called *Results* and the chart is on a worksheet called *Risk Chart*.

The file can be found on the CD accompanying this book under the name **RISK**.

Changing the original plan

Two changes are required to the basic plan. These are for the input form to accommodate ranges of data and for the logic of the plan to incorporate a random number generator using the range data.

The selection of the data for insertion in the plan is based on either a probability distribution, or in the case of the risk analysis described in this book, a random number generator. The specification of probability distributions for risk analysis is beyond the scope of this book, and thus it is assumed that the data will be specified as simple maximum and minimum values and that all possible obtainable results are of equal probability. This is referred to in statistical jargon as *rectangular distributions*.

Figure 13.1 shows the data input form for risk analysis on the Capital Investment Appraisal model. For this example the variable data is the investment amount, the cash-in flows, the fixed and the inflation adjusted discount rates. An option for performing risk analysis on three variables has been given. These are NPV at a fixed interest rate, IRR and NPV at a variable discount rate.

Cells and ranges in the output selection part of the input form need to be named for future reference in the *Results* sheet. Therefore using the Insert Name Define command in Excel or the Range Name command in 1-2-3 names representing the three variables that the risk analysis can be performed on are assigned as follows:

E17   NPVF
E18   IRR
E19   NPVV

	A	B	C	D	E	F	G	H	I	J	K	L	M
1	Input form for Risk Analysis												
2				Minimum	Maximum								
3	IT Investment - Cash Out			350000	400000								
4													
5	Net IT Benefits	Year 1		60000	70000								
6		Year 2		95000	105000								
7		Year 3		120000	130000								
8		Year 4		180000	200000								
9		Year 5		200000	250000								
10													
11	Fixed Cost of Capital			20.00%	30.00%								
12													
13	Inflation adjusted cost of capital			Y1 Min	Y1 Max	Y2 Min	Y2 Max	Y3 Min	Y3 Max	Y4 Min	Y4 Max	Y5 Min	Y5 Max
14				20%	25%	30%	35%	35%	40%	40%	45%	45%	50%
15													
16													
17	Select variable to report				NPV (FDR)	-67077							
18	with an X in the appropriate box			X	IRR	19.85%							
19					NPV (VDR)	-86502							
20													
21			N.B. You must mark ONLY ONE box with an upper case X										
22													
23													

CIA Model / Risk Model \ Input / Results / Riskchart / Sheet5 / Sheet6

Ready — Sum=0

Figure 13.1 Input form for risk analysis

References to the formulae for these variables in the main model on the *Risk Model* sheet should be entered into cells F17, F18 and F19 as follows:

	EXCEL	1-2-3
F17	='Risk Model'!C19	+Risk Model:C19
F18	='Risk Model'!C21	+Risk Model:C21
F19	='Risk Model'!C24	+Risk Model:C24

At this point cells F17, F18 and F19 will be displaying the current values for the net present vale, the internal rate of return and the net present value at a variable discount rate. As it is not necessary for the user to see the value in these cells selecting them and changing the font colour to white can hide them.

The range D17 through F19 is named LOOKTAB and will be referenced as a lookup table in the *Results* sheet.

Incorporating the RAND function

In order to select values at random from within the specified ranges the referencing cells in the main model use the RAND function in the following way:

INT(RAND * (MAXIMUM − MINIMUM) + MINIMUM)

The RAND function generates a value between 0 and 1, never actually being 0 or 1. Looking at Figure 13.1 the range of values for the investment has been specified as between 350,000 and 400,000 and so if RAND returned a value of .56125, the above formula would calculate as:

INTEGER of .56125 * (400000 −350000) + 350000

which will give an answer of 378,062. In fact the result will always be a value between the specified ranges.

Figure 13.2 shows some of the formulae in the main model incorporating the random number generator. The formulae are the same for Excel and 1-2-3 although the form of the RAND in Excel is RAND() as opposed to @RAND in 1-2-3.

	A	B	C
1	Capital Investment Appraisal System		
2			
3		Cash-Out	Cash-In
4	IT Investment - Cash Out	=INT(RAND()*(Input!E3-Input!D3)+Input!D3)	
5	Net IT Benefits Year 1		=INT(RAND()*(Input!E5-Input!D5)+Input!D5)
6	Year 2		=INT(RAND()*(Input!E6-Input!D6)+Input!D6)
7	Year 3		=INT(RAND()*(Input!E7-Input!D7)+Input!D7)
8	Year 4		=INT(RAND()*(Input!E8-Input!D8)+Input!D8)
9	Year 5		=INT(RAND()*(Input!E9-Input!D9)+Input!D9)
10			
11	Fixed Cost of Capital or Interest Rate		=(RAND()*(Input!E11-Input!D11)+Input!D11)
12			
13			Y1
14	Forecast inflation rates		=RAND()*(Input!E14-Input!D14)+Input!D14
15			
16	Investment Reports on IT System		
17	Payback in years & months		=B37
18	Rate of return(%)		=AVERAGE(C5:C9)/ABS(B4)
19	N P V Fixed Discount Rate (FDR)		=NPV(C11,C5:C9)-B4
20	Profitability Index FDR (PI)		=NPV(C11,C5:C9)/B4
21	Internal Rate of Return (IRR)		=IRR(E4:E9,0.3)
22			

Figure 13.2 Incorporating a random number generator

The system generates a different random number every time the spreadsheet is recalculated and thus by pressing F9 a different set of values will be returned in the main model and in turn the investment reports will be recalculated using different data each time.

The results worksheet

The results of recalculating the model are collected on the *results* worksheet together with some summary statistics and a frequency distribution table. Figure 13.3 shows the Excel *results* sheet.

	A	B	C	D	E	F	G	H
1	Risk analysis results - Press F9 to recalculate							
2								
3		IRR		Summary statistics for	IRR		Frequency Table	
4		0.17						IRR
5	1	0.21		Mean	0.20		0.164	1
6	2	0.21		Standard Deviation	0.02		0.172	30
7	3	0.22		Range	0.08		0.180	124
8	4	0.21		Minimum	0.16		0.188	257
9	5	0.22		Maximum	0.24		0.196	290
10	6	0.21		Count	2000.00		0.204	289
11	7	0.23					0.212	321
12	8	0.22					0.219	315
13	9	0.18					0.227	233
14	10	0.23					0.235	113
15	11	0.20					0.243	27
16	12	0.22						

Figure 13.3 Results worksheet

In order that the risk analysis will be performed on the variable marked with an X on the Input worksheet, formulae are required in cells B3 and B4. A VLOOKUP function is used is both cases. Cell B3 is a reference to the variable label and the following formula is required:

For Excel:

=IF(ISERR(VLOOKUP("X",looktab,2)),"Make a selection",
    VLOOKUP("X",looktab,2))

For 1-2-3:

@IF(ISERR(VLOOKUP("X",looktab,1)),"Make a selection",
    VLOOKUP("X",looktab,1))

The VLOOKUP in this formula looks for X in the first column of the table range *looktab* and returns the contents of the cell one column to the right. (Note that LOOKUP functions are case sensitive which is why it is necessary to ensure that X is entered in upper case.)

However, if something other than upper case X is entered the VLOOKUP function will return an error. For this reason the formula begins with ISERR which means that if the result of the VLOOKUP is an error the text "Make a selection" will be returned, otherwise the result VLOOKUP function will be returned, which in the case of Figure 13.3 is IRR.

A similar formula is required in cell B4 to pick up the cell reference to the variable data which in the case of Figure 13.3 is 0.18:

For Excel:

=VLOOKUP("X",looktab,3)

For 1-2-3:

@VLOOKUP("X",looktab,2)

The labels in cells E3 and H4 are simple references to cell B4.

Collecting the results

The results of the risk analysis will be collected using a data or what-if table. The more reiterations of the model the better the results, and so for this example the plan has been set up to perform 2000 recalculations, thus collecting 2000 different results. Numbers 1 through 2000 are entered into cells A5 through A2004. To calculate the table the range A4 through B2004 is highlighted and the Table command selected by Data Table in Excel and Range Analyse What-if in 1-2-3. This is a 1-way table requiring Column input and the reference can be to any blank cell, such as A3. When OK is clicked the table is calculated by placing the number 1 in cell A3, recalculating the model and placing the IRR in cell B5. The number 2 is then entered in cell A3, the model is recalculated, which due to the RAND function causes all input and output to change and the new IRR is placed in cell B6. The computer continues this process 2000 times at which point there are 2000 IRR results in the range B5 through B2004.

Note that in Excel it is important at this point to set recalculation to Automatic except Tables from the Tools Calculation box otherwise the table will be recalculated every time something is entered into the spreadsheet. This is not necessary in 1-2-3 as the results of the table is data as opposed to formulae.

Summary statistics

Some useful statistics about the results have been entered into the range D5 through E10. To make the referencing of the data easier the range B5 through B2004 is named OUTPUT and the following formulae are required in column E:

E5	AVERAGE(output)
E6	STDEV(output)
E7	E9–E8
E8	MIN(output)
E9	MAX(output)
E10	COUNT(output)

The results of the risk analysis are most clearly viewed graphically, but 2000 data point is too many to plot onto a graph. Therefore a frequency distribution of the data is created and a graph drawn using this data.

For this example 11 data points have been chosen, beginning with the minimum value returned as a result and then 10 further points at equal intervals finishing with the maximum value returned as a result. This is achieved with the following formulae in cells G5 and G6:

G5	E8
G6	G5+($E$7*0.1)

The formula in cell G6 is then copied to cell G15.

Frequency distribution with Excel

The FREQUENCY function is used to return the number of times the results fall between the specified ranges. The form of the FREQUENCY command in cell H5 is:

={FEQUENCY(B5:B2004,G5:G15)}

The {} brackets mean this is an *array* function and as such has to be entered in a special way. First select the range in which the formulae is required – H5 through H15. Then enter the formula *without* the {} brackets. Then enter the formula by holding the CTRL key and pressing SHIFT ENTER. The full range will be calculated in one operation.

Frequency distribution with 1-2-3

There is no function for creating a frequency distribution in 1-2-3 and the command is accessed by selecting Range Analyse Distribution and then specifying the data range which is OUTPUT and the *bin* range which is G5…G15.

To automate the process for repeated use of the model a small macro can be recorded with this command sequence which can be assigned to a button as shown in Figure 13.4.

	A	B	C	D	E	F	G	H
1	Risk analysis results - Press F8 to recalculate						Press to calc freq. dist.	
2								
3			IRR	Summary statistics for	IRR		Frequency Table	
4			0.21					IRR
5		1	0.21	Mean	0.20		0.17	1
6		2	0.19	Standard Deviation	0.02		0.17	37
7		3	0.20	Range	0.08		0.18	147
8		4	0.19	Minimum	0.17		0.19	287
9		5	0.20	Maximum	0.25		0.20	334
10		6	0.22	Count	2000.00		0.21	325
11		7	0.20				0.21	314
12		8	0.21				0.22	283
13		9	0.19				0.23	196
14		10	0.18				0.24	69
15		11	0.22				0.25	7
16		12	0.22					0
17		13	0.19					
18		14	0.21					

Figure 13.4 1-2-3 results sheet

Details of how the macro is created can be seen by looking at the model supplied on the disk.

The results in Figure 13.4 are not exactly the same as those shown in Figure 13.3 because the RAND function will generate different values each time. Similarly readers who try this exercise themselves, or use the plan supplied on the accompanying disk will never have exactly the same results.

Displaying the results graphically

The results can be displayed graphically by selecting the range G4 through H15 and using the Chart button to automatically create a chart such as the one shown in Figure 13.5.

This graph illustrates quite a low level of risk because the most likely outcome is a return of 21.20% with a standard deviation of 1.6%. Furthermore even if all the most unfavourable estimates occur, i.e. maximum investment costs, lowest cash-in flows and highest cost of capital, this investment will still be expected to produce an IRR of 16.4%. On the other hand if the investment is kept low and the highest cash-in flows are achieved with a low cost of capital, this investment could produce a return of 24.3%.

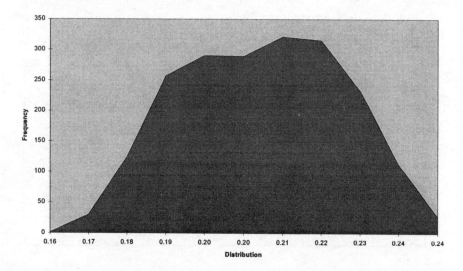

Figure 13.5 Graphical results of risk analysis on IRR

Using the risk analysis model

Having set the risk analysis model up as shown in this Chapter it can be used with different ranges of input data, in this example to analyse varying investment amounts with different cash flow and discount rate scenarios. By putting an X in the appropriate box in the input sheet the analysis can be performed on the NPV at a fixed discount rate, the IRR or the NPV at a variable discount rate. If it is only appropriate to specify ranges for some of the input variables the same value can be entered for the minimum and maximum in the input sheet.

To recalculate the model after new input data has been entered or a different output variable has been selected F9 is pressed in Excel and F8 in 1-2-3 which forces the table to recalculate and the remaining formulae cells are also re-evaluated. To update the frequency distribution table in 1-2-3 the command or macro must be executed.

SUMMARY

The risk of any investment is the potential for input and/or output variables to fluctuate from their original estimates. Risk analysis accommodates this uncertainty by allowing ranges, as opposed to single point estimates, to be used. It is generally easier to confidently state that an investment will be between 300,000 and 400,000 than to say it will be 380,000.

The methodology applied to this example can be used with most well-designed deterministic plans.

14

Part Three

Budgeting

You can fool all the people all the time if the advertising is right and the budget is big enough.

Joseph E. Levine, U.S. film producer, executive. Quoted in: *Halliwell's Filmgoer's Companion*, 1984.

INTRODUCTION

A budget is a detailed estimate of future transactions. It can be expressed in terms of physical quantities, money, or both. The essence of a budget is that it is a target set for management to achieve or surpass. Thus a budget is always associated with a specific departmental responsibility point or centre within the firm. This might be a division that has a sales budget, a factory with a capital budget, or an individual with an expense budget. Whatever the case, there will normally be an individual responsible for achieving the budget.

SCOPE OF BUDGETING

Budgetary control is not limited to commercial and industrial firms attempting to produce a profit. The procedures involved are equally applicable to *not for profit* organisations such as government departments, universities and charities.

All aspects of the business or organisation can be budgeted. There might be *income and expenditure* budgets, *cash* budgets, *capital* budgets, *research and development* budgets to mention only a few examples. Budgets can be classified as *master* budgets, *departmental* budgets or *functional* budgets. Whatever level or degree of detail, a budget is useless if it does not focus on a point of responsibility.

Budgeting is a management function that incorporates:

1. setting objectives;
2. establishing detailed financial estimates;
3. delegating specific responsibility;
4. monitoring performance;
5. reacting to expectations.

BENEFITS OF BUDGETING

The benefits of budgetary control can usefully be classified in the following way:

1. a budget forces management to express in figures its future intentions;
2. it provides a yardstick by which individuals or groups can be measured and rewarded;
3. it allows some responsibility and authority to be decentralised without loss of information required by management for control purposes;
4. budgeting provides a mechanism to control in detail the revenue, costs, cash and capital expenditure of the firm;
5. it facilitates an atmosphere of cost consciousness;

6. it helps ensure that return on investment is optimised.

DIFFERENT APPROACHES TO BUDGETING

There are various approaches to the preparation of a budgeting system, but two popular methods are the *traditional approach* and the *zero-based budgeting approach*.

With the traditional approach some firms simply re-compile last year's or the previous period's figures, adjusted for expected growth, or for inflation. This approach to formulating a budget relies on the notion that all the business variables will remain more or less the same in relationship to one another from one period to the next. For this type of budget, after preparing an initial set of figures, a minimal amount of preparation is required.

Some firms adopt the view that the most important aspect of budgetary control lies in the fact that the creation of budgets should impose on the firm a *strict regime of thinking through* what the firm is doing and where it is going. This approach has been popularised under the title of zero-based budgeting (ZBB) and assumes that it is necessary to start the budgeting process from scratch each time. The main advantage of this approach is that is ensures a rethink of the basic business assumptions on which the firm relies. With a ZBB system, each functional section in the business will plan in detail all revenue, expenditure and capital items and these items will be ranked in order of importance to the firm.

An outcome from a ZBB system that is not the case with the traditional approach is that management are forced to prove the need for each item of expenditure in the budget. It is not good enough to say that the promotion account had a particular amount in it last year and that this figure should be increased by 10% for inflation. Clearly it is more expensive to operate a ZBB system than a traditional system, and therefore a cost benefit study is appropriate before embarking on a ZBB.

The term ZBB is generally associated with the budgeting of indirect costs. It is therefore used extensively in central service departments, marketing and distribution, and research and development. ZBB is not considered to be directly relevant to the manufacturing process, as detailed expenditure in this area is usually automatically accounted for on a variable or direct basis.

BUDGET PREPARATION

The procedure and operation of any budgetary control system is clearly specific to each individual organisation and is a function of management style and corporate culture. However, there are general guidelines that are useful to bear in mind:

1. Establishing the firms' objectives. This usually involves a lengthy process of analysing the firms' strengths and weaknesses and matching these to the opportunities in the environment in which the firm functions. This is sometimes referred to as *strategic planning*. This is a senior management activity which is an ongoing process coming to a focal point at budget time. A top-down approach is normally dominant here.

2. Forecasting the key business variables. Before any figures can be derived an activity forecast must be established. In many organisations this means that a sales forecast must be produced which can be a lengthy and difficult process. It is important to ensure that a broad spectrum of people are involved and committed to the sales forecast. Therefore both top-down and bottom-up approaches are appropriate here.

3. Physical estimates are calculated. The number of people, the scale of equipment and the volumes of raw materials required must be established. This is usually a bottom-up procedure.

4. Detailed costings of each responsibility centre are made. This requires the involvement of a wide variety of staff and can lead to a considerable amount of negotiation. Thus both top-down and bottom-up approaches are required.

These activities are best conducted in a cyclical fashion with feedback being sent up and down the organisation at various times, representing how different groups feel about the suggestions being made. Thus the amount of time required to produce a budget can be substantial.

SPREADSHEETS FOR BUDGETS

A spreadsheet can be used to support both the traditional approach to budgeting as well as the zero-based approach.

With the traditional approach, having initially designed and developed a plan with care, continuous use of the system is largely a case of changing the input data. Template techniques shown in Chapter 9 are invaluable in this situation.

Templates can also form the basis of zero-based budgets as, even when starting from scratch, an outline of the requirements for the budget is known and a template can form the basis of the new budget.

SUMMARY

Budgeting is an essential part of modern management and is regularly performed in most organisations. It is as much a management philosophy and technique as an approach to financial accounting.

The spreadsheet is a particularly powerful tool in the development of budgets. It is also useful for the production of reports such as budget–actual–variance, year-to-date totals and consolidated results.

A Spreadsheet Budgeting System

It is a mistake to look too far ahead. Only one link in the chain of destiny can be handled at a time.

Anonymous

INTRODUCTION

The budgetary control system described in this chapter illustrates how files can be linked in order to provide a flexible reporting facility. Figure 15.1 shows the modules of the system. The system is a quarterly plan for a single department or division and provides for the collection of quarterly budget figures and actual values. Options for producing variance reports and year-to-date reports are provided.

Rather than develop a large file with the different modules on separate sheets, different files for each module will be created for this example. There are both advantages and disadvantages to linking data across files. One of the main advantages is that different parts of a system can be worked on simultaneously by different people. Probably the most significant disadvantage is that when there are many files to link the formulae can become very long and complex.

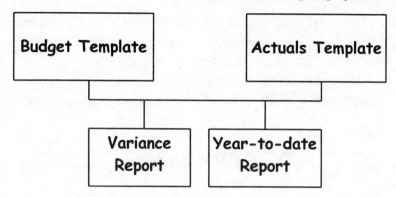

Figure 15.1 Proposed budgetary control system

When embarking on a spreadsheet system that links cells across files it is advisable to keep the files in the same directory. The reason for this is that the spreadsheet keeps a track of the directory path when the links are established and problems can arise if files are moved, directory names or filenames are changed[1].

For the purposes of explaining how to develop a linked spreadsheet system for budgetary control a small summary profit and loss account will be used as the basis for the budget. Obviously in a real situation the files will be larger, but the methodology is the same. The system is supplied on the CD accompanying this book in a separate directory called **BUDGET**. The system then comprises three files called **BUDGET**, **ACTUALS** and **VARIANCE**.

PREPARING THE BUDGET TEMPLATE

The summary profit and loss account is a deterministic model. Figure 15.2 shows the results of the plan after some data has been entered and Figure 15.3 is the data input form. This model has been designed following using the template methodology described in Chapter 9 and has two sheets. The first is called *Budget* and contains the logic for the plan and the second is called *Input* and consists of the data input form. The file is saved with the name

---

[1] For this reason readers wishing to use the system supplied on the accompanying disk should load the files from the floppy disk. If it is necessary to use the files from a hard disk it will be necessary to select Edit Links and change the path reference accordingly.

BUDGET. Although any name can be used it is important to carefully select the required name, as the other files will reference it in the system. Once the budgetary control system is complete the four files can be saved as template files with an XLT or WKT extension in order that they can be used repeatedly for different sets of data.

	A	B	C	D	E	F
1	Budget for 199X					
2						
3		Qtr1	Qtr2	Qtr3	Qtr4	Total
4	Sales	8000	8080	8161	8242	32483
5	Unit Price	37.50	37.69	37.88	38.07	
6	Revenue	300000	304515	309098	313750	1227363
7						
8	Direct Costs	6000	6090	6182	6275	24547
9						
10	Gross Profit	294000	298425	302916	307475	1202816
11						
12	Overheads	15000	15150	15302	15455	60906
13						
14	Net Profit	279000	283275	287614	292020	1141910

Figure 15.1 Budget plan with data

	A	B	C	D	E
1	Budget input form				
2					
3		Opening Value	Growth Rate	Opening Proportion	
4					
5	Sales	8000	1.00%		
6	Unit Price	37.5	0.50%		
7					
8	Direct Costs			2.00%	of turnover
9	Overhead Costs	15000	1.00%		
10					

Figure 15.2 Data input form for budget plan

Once completed this file is saved with the name BUDGET.

PREPARING THE ACTUAL TEMPLATE

To minimise the work required for the Actual file, open BUDGET, copy columns A and B to a new file, remove any existing data and shade the cells into which input is required. Figure 15.3 shows the first sheet of the Actual file. As this is a quarterly plan it has to be possible to enter four separate sets of actual data. Therefore the information in Figure 15.3 is copied into three further sheets and the sheets are names QTR1, QTR2, QTR3 and QTR4 respectively. To clarify which sheet is which the title of each sheet is also labelled as can be seen from Figure 15.3.

	A	B	C
1	Actual data for Quarter		1
2			
3			
4	Sales	8100	
5	Unit Price	37.50	
6	Revenue	303750	
7			
8	Direct Costs	130000	
9			
10	Gross Profit	173750	
11			
12	Overheads	12000	
13			
14	Net Profit	161750	
15			
16			
17			
18			
19			
20			
21			
22			
23			

Qtr1 / Qtr2 / Qtr3 / Qtr4 / Sheet6

Figure 15.3 Template for Actual data with
sample data for first quarter

Once completed the actuals template is saved in the same directory as BUDGET with the name ACTUAL.

PREPARING THE VARIANCE REPORT TEMPLATE

The variance report requires the user to select a quarter for which a report is required. The system will then select the appropriate range from the budget file and the actual file.

Figure 15.4 shows a variance report for the first quarter using the data for the first quarter's budget shown in Figure 15.1 and the actual data shown in Figure 15.3.

	A	B	C	D
1	Variance report for Quarter			1
2				
3		Budget	Actual	Variance
4	Sales	8000	8100	-100
5	Unit Price	37.50	37.50	0.00
6	Revenue	300000	303750	-3750
7				
8	Direct Costs	6000	130000	-124000
9				
10	Gross Profit	294000	173750	120250
11				
12	Overheads	15000	12000	3000
13				
14	Net Profit	279000	161750	117250

Figure 15.4 Example variance report

The user enters the required quarter number in cell D1 and the following nested IF function is required in cell B4 to pick up the appropriate data.

In Excel:

```
=IF($D$1=1,[Budget.xls]Budgets!B4,IF($D$1=2,[Budget.xls]Budgets!C4,
    IF($D$1=3,[Budget.xls]Budgets!D4,IF($D$1=4,[Budget.xls]Budgets!
        E4,"!!!"))))
```

In 1-2-3:

```
@IF($D$1=1,<<Budget.WK4>>Budgets:B4..Budgets:B4,@IF($D$1=2,
   <<Budget.WK4>>Budgets:C4..Budgets:C4,@IF($D$1=3,
      <<Budget.WK4>>Budgets:D4..Budgets:D4,@IF($D$1=4,
         <<Budget.WK4>>Budgets:E4..Budgets:E4,"!!!"))))
```

This formula can be copied to the remaining cells in the budget column of the variance report.

If a number other than 1 to 4 is entered the above formula will return !!! in the cell. In addition the following IF function has been entered into cell E1:

In Excel:

```
=IF(OR(D1<1,D1>4),"Enter a quarter number between 1 and 4","")
```

In 1-2-3:

```
@IF(((D1<1)#OR#(D1>4)),"Enter a quarter number between 1 and 4","")
```

A formula similar to that used for the budgets is required for the actual column of the variance report, but with a reference to the appropriate sheet of the ACTUAL file. The formula in cell C4 is therefore:

In Excel:

```
=IF($D$1=1,[Actual.xls]Qtr1!B4,IF($D$1=2,[Actual.xls]Qtr2!B4,IF($D$1=3,
   [Actual.xls]Qtr3!B4,IF($D$1=4,[Actual.xls]Qtr4!B4,"!!!"))))
```

In 1-2-3:

```
@IF($D$1=1,<<Actual.WK4>>Qtr1:B4..Qtr1:B4,@IF($D$1=2,
   <<Actual.WK4>>Qtr2:B4..Qtr2:B4,@IF($D$1=3,<<Actual.WK4>>
      Qtr3:B4..Qtr3:B4,@IF($D$1=4,<<Actual.WK4>>
         Qtr4:B4..Qtr4:B4,"!!!"))))
```

This formula can be copied for the remaining cells in column C. To complete the variance report the actual data is subtracted from the budget data.

PREPARING THE YEAR-TO-DATE REPORT TEMPLATE

The variance report is designed to calculate the variance for any given quarter. However it is also useful to have a year-to-date report that shows the cumulative variance for a specified number of quarters.

Figure 15.5 shows a year-to-date variance report for two quarters.

	A	B	C	D	E	F	G	H	I
1	Year-to-date report for how many quarters?				2		No data for quarter	3	Actuals
2									
3		Budget	Actual	Variance					
4	Sales	16080	16600	-520					
5	Average Unit Price	37.59	39.80	-2					
6	Revenue	604515	660750	-56235					
7									
8	Direct Costs	241806	210000	31806					
9									
10	Gross Profit	362709	450750	-88041					
11									
12	Overheads	30150	27000	3150					
13									
14	Net Profit	332559	423750	-91191					
15									

Figure 15.5 Year-to-date variance report for two quarters

This report works by adding together the budget and actual data for the number of quarters that are specified in cell E1. As the actual data is only added to the file when it becomes available cell H1 reports the first quarter for which there is no data. Therefore with the above example it is only possible to prepare a year-to-date report for the first or second quarters as there is not yet any data available for the third quarter.

The following formula is required in cell H1 which will report the first quarter in which there is no actual data. If there is data in all four quarters the cell will remain blank. This is achieved through the use of the "" at the end of the formula:

In Excel:

```
=IF([Actual.xls]Qtr1!$B$4=0,1,IF([Actual.xls]Qtr2!$B$4=0,2,
    IF([Actual.xls]Qtr3!$B$4=0,3,IF([Actual.xls]Qtr4!$B$4=0,4,""))))
```

In 1-2-3:

```
@IF(<<actual.wk4>>$Qtr1:$B$4..$Qtr1:$B$4=0,1,
    @IF(<<actual.wk4>>$Qtr2:$B$4..$Qtr2:$B$4=0,2,
        @IF(<<actual.wk4>>$Qtr3:$B$4..$Qtr3:$B$4=0,3,
            @IF(<<actual.wk4>>$Qtr4:$B$4..$Qtr4:$B$4=0,4,""))))
```

The following formula is required in cell B4 to produce the year-to-date budget amount based on the number of quarters entered into cell E1.

In Excel:

```
=IF($E$1=1,[Budget.xls]Budgets!B4,IF($E$1=2,SUM
    ([Budget.xls]Budgets!B4:C4),IF($E$1=3,SUM([Budget.xls]Budgets!
    B4:D4),IF($E$1=4,SUM([Budget.xls]Budgets!B4:E4),"!!!"))))
```

In 1-2-3:

```
IF($E$1=1,<<Budget.WK4>>Budgets:B4..Budgets:B4,@IF($E$1=2,
    @SUM(<<Budget.WK4>>Budgets:B4..Budgets:C4),@IF($E$1=3,
        @SUM(<<Budget.WK4>>Budgets:B4..Budgets:D4),@IF($E$1=4,
            @SUM(<<Budget.WK4>>Budgets:B4..Budgets:E4),"!!!"))))
```

If a number other than 1, 2, 3 or 4 is entered into cell E1 the above formula will return !!!, alerting the user to the fact that a valid quarter number has not been entered. This formula can be copied to the remaining cells in the budget column, with the exception of the unit price. It is not appropriate to accumulate a unit price and therefore the average unit price is calculated in cell B5 by dividing the revenue by the sales.

A formula similar to that used to calculate the year-to-date budgets is required for the actuals as shown below:

In Excel:

```
=IF($E$1>=$H$1,"No data",IF($E$1=1,[Actual.xls]Qtr1!B4,
    IF($E$1=2,SUM([Actual.xls]Qtr1:Qtr2!B4:B4),IF($E$1=3,
        SUM([Actual.xls]Qtr1:Qtr4!B4:B4),IF($E$1=4,
            SUM([Actual.xls]Qtr1:Qtr4!B4:B4),"!!!")))))
```

In 1-2-3:

```
@IF($E$1>=$H$1,"No data",@IF($E$1=1,<<Actual.WK4>>
    Qtr1:B5..Qtr1:B5,@IF($E$1=2,@SUM(<<Actual.WK4>>
        Qtr1:B5..Qtr2:B5),@IF($E$1=3,@SUM(<<Actual.WK4>>
            Qtr1:B5..Qtr3:B5),@IF($E$1=4,@SUM(<<Actual.WK4>>
                Qtr1:B5..Qtr4:B5),"!!!")))))
```

The first part of the above formula compares the number of quarters entered into cell E1 with cell H1 which is reporting the actuals quarter for which there is no data. If E1 is greater than or equal to H1 the message "No data" is returned, otherwise the appropriate number of periods are accumulated.

As with the budget column the formula can be copied to the remaining cells, but again the unit price is changed to be the average unit price by dividing the revenue by the sales.

The year-to-date variance is calculated in the same way as in the variance report by subtracting the year-to-date actuals from the year-to-date budgets. An enhancement is made to this formula to check the contents of actuals in order that the variance will be left blank if the "No data" message is returned for the actual. Therefore the following formula is entered in cell D4 and copied for the remaining cells in the variance column.

In Excel:

=IF(C4="No data","",B4–C4)

In 1-2-3:

@IF(C4="No data","",B4–C4)

SUMMARY

The four files that have been developed in this chapter describe a methodology for producing a flexible budgetary control system. The flexibility is primarily due to the use of separate files for each module of the system which means that different people can work on different parts of the system at the same time and users can choose to produce reports using selected data.

Before using the system it is important to ensure that all the files are in the same directory and that the links are correctly referencing the files. It might be necessary to select Edit Links and amend the path if the system is installed on another user's computer.

Consolidating Data

Man is still the most extraordinary computer of all.

John F. Kennedy (1917–1963), U.S. Democratic politician, president. Speech, 21 May 1963.

INTRODUCTION

The budgetary control system described in Chapter 15 was for a single division or department. In many organisations it is necessary to consolidate, summate or aggregate the data from separate divisions to produce a divisional or corporate report.

The consolidation options available in the spreadsheet allow for selected ranges of data from different files to be merged into a single file with options for summing, subtracting, averaging etc.

To illustrate the consolidation features the variance report from the budgetary control system will be used. As the commands required to combine files and parts of files differ from spreadsheet to spreadsheet, the procedure for Excel and 1-2-3 will be described separately.

CONSOLIDATING DATA WITH EXCEL

Excel provides a powerful set of consolidation tools through the Data Consolidate command. However, before using the command a set of files to be consolidated need to be created. To do this open the *Variance* file and select a valid quarter number in order to produce a variance report. To simplify the consolidation procedure the range to be included in the consolidation is named by selecting the range A3:D14 followed by Insert Name Define and call the range Data_Area.

To indicate that this is a variance report for a division enter *Division A* into cell A2 and then save the file as DIVA. To quickly produce another two files for this consolidation exercise change the division reference in cell B2 to *Division B* and save the file as DIVB and then change B2 once more to *Division C* and save the file as DIVC.

The next step is to create a new file that will form the consolidated report. Type an appropriate title for the report into cell A1 and then place the cursor on the cell that will be the top left cell of the consolidated range, which for this example will be B3.

Select Data Consolidate, which produces the dialogue box shown in Figure 16.1. The default function for the consolidate command is SUM, i.e. the corresponding cells from the selected ranges will be summed. However by clicking on the arrow to the right of the function box the other alternatives can be seen.

The reference box refers to the files or ranges that are to be consolidated. To complete this click on Browse and select the file DIVA. After the exclamation mark (!) type the range name Data_area and then change the *A* in *DivA* to a question mark (?). This is a wildcard that will replace any single character for the question mark. Click Add to put this reference in the list of references to be consolidated. The effect of this reference is that when the OK button is clicked the system will open each file beginning with DIV and take the range in those files called Data_area and sum them into the current worksheet. The range Data_area does not have to be in the same position in each file, but it should be the same area in each file in order that the correct cells are added together.

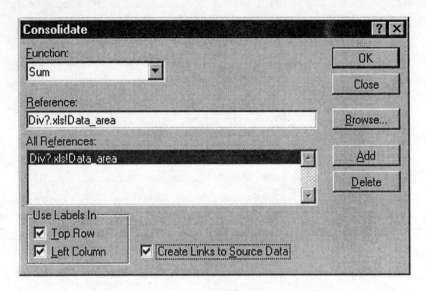

Figure 16.1 Data consolidate dialogue box

It is not always possible to name files and ranges with similar names and if this is the case each file and range to be consolidated must be individually selected and the *Add* box checked until the full list is displayed in the dialogue box. To illustrate this Figure 16.2 shows a completed dialogue box referencing the files separately with range references instead of the common range name.

Before clicking OK, check the three boxes at the bottom of the dialogue box to indicate that the top row and left column of the ranges to be consolidated are labels and that links are required to the source files. Figure 16.3 shows the results of the consolidation.

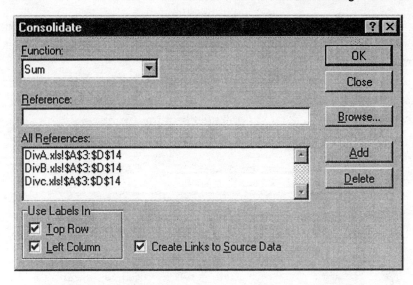

Figure 16.2 Consolidate dialogue box with separate references

1 2		A	B	C	D	E
	1	Consolidated Variance Report				
	2					
	3			Budget	Actual	Variance
+	7	Sales		24240	25500	-1260
+	11	Unit Price		113.06	126.00	-12.94
+	15	Revenue		913545	1071000	-157455
+	19	Direct Costs		365418	240000	125418
+	23	Gross Profit		548127	831000	-282873
+	27	Overheads		45450	45000	450
+	31	Net Profit		502677	786000	-283323
	32					

Figure 16.3 Results of Data Consolidate command

Because the *Create links to source data* box was checked in the dialogue box the bar to the left of the report is automatically produced. By clicking on the number 2 the report is expanded as shown in Figure 16.4. This shows the data from all the ranges included in the Consolidate command.

Looking at the data in Figure 16.3 the references to the three divisional files show the full path to those files and the totals contain a SUM function.

It is useful to be able to audit the source data of a consolidated report, but if a large number of files are being consolidated it may represent too much data. By not selecting the *Create links to source data* box, only the results will be produced in the consolidated report.

1 2		A	B	C	D	E
	1	Consolidated Variance Report				
	2					
	3			Budget	Actual	Variance
	4		Diva	8080	8500	-420
	5		Divb	8080	8500	-420
	6		Divc	8080	8500	-420
	7	Sales		24240	25500	-1260
	8		Diva	37.69	42.00	-4.31
	9		Divb	37.69	42.00	-4.31
	10		Divc	37.69	42.00	-4.31
	11	Unit Price		113.06	126.00	-12.94
	12		Diva	304515	357000	-52485
	13		Divb	304515	357000	-52485
	14		Divc	304515	357000	-52485
	15	Revenue		913545	1071000	-157455
	16		Diva	121806	80000	41806
	17		Divb	121806	80000	41806
	18		Divc	121806	80000	41806
	19	Direct Costs		365418	240000	125418
	20		Diva	182709	277000	-94291
	21		Divb	182709	277000	-94291
	22		Divc	182709	277000	-94291
	23	Gross Profit		548127	831000	-282873
	24		Diva	15150	15000	150

Figure 16.4 Expanded consolidated report

CONSOLIDATING DATA WITH 1-2-3

Cells from different files can be added together in 1-2-3 through the File Open Combine command. Before using the command a set of files to be consolidated need to be created. To do this open the

VARIANCE file and select a valid quarter number in order to produce a variance report. To simplify the consolidation procedure the range to be included in the consolidation is named by selecting the range B4:D14, followed by Range Name and call the range Data_area. It is important that only the data is included in the name and not the row or column headings.

To indicate that this is a variance report for a division enter *Division A* into cell A2 and then save the file as DIVA. To quickly produce another two files for this consolidation exercise change the division reference in cell B2 to *Division B* and save the file as DIVB and then change B2 once more to *Division C* and save the file as DIVC.

The next step is to create a template that will form the consolidated report. This file needs to have the column and row headings that correspond with the data that will be consolidated. The quick way to produce this template is to once again open the *Variance* file and then delete all the data and formulae, leaving only the headings in place. This file, which has been saved as CONSOL is shown in Figure 16.5.

A	A	B	C	D
1	Consolidated variance report			
2				
3		Budget	Actual	Variance
4	Sales			
5	AverageUnit Price			
6	Revenue			
7				
8	Direct Costs			
9				
10	Gross Profit			
11				
12	Overheads			
13				
14	Net Profit			

Figure 16.5 Template for consolidated report

The cursor must be positioned on the cell that corresponds with the top left cell of the range to be consolidated. Therefore for this example place the cursor on cell B4.

The first file to be included in the consolidation can now be added to the template with the command File Open, select the file DIVA and then click on Combine which produces the dialogue box shown in Figure 16.6.

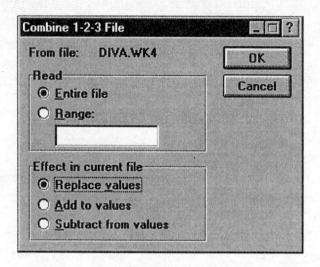

Figure 16.6 File combine dialogue box

In this example it is the range named Data_area that is to be added and so this is entered into the range box and then it is important to check the Add to values box before clicking on OK.

This procedure is repeated for the other two divisional files, DIVB and DIVC.

The range Data_area included the unit price, which has therefore also been added together. After adding in the file DIVC the unit price is changed to the average unit price by dividing the Revenue by the Sales. Figure 16.7 shows the resulting consolidated report.

	A	B	C	D
1	Consolidated variance report			
2				
3		Budget	Actual	Variance
4	Sales	24240	25500	-1260
5	AverageUnit Price	38	42	-12.94
6	Revenue	913545	1071000	-157455
7				
8	Direct Costs	365418	240000	125418
9				
10	Gross Profit	548127	831000	-282873
11				
12	Overheads	45450	45000	450
13				
14	Net Profit	502677	786000	-283323
15				

Figure 16.7 Completed consolidated report

SUMMARY

The spreadsheet consolidate options provide a means of adding data together from different files without the need for linking files. This is especially useful when a large number of files need to be accessed as the file linking procedures require long formulae and take time to recalculate.

The examples shown in this chapter can be further automated through the use of macros in order that, especially in 1-2-3, the user does not have to enter the information for each file to be included in the consolidated report.

Index